Texts in Computing

Volume 1

Programming Languages
and
Operational Semantics

An Introduction

Volume 1
Programming Languages and Operational Semantics: An Introduction
Maribel Fernández

Volume 2
An Introduction to Lambda Calculi for Computer Scientists
Chris Hankin

Volume 3
Logical Reasoning: A First Course
Rob Nederpelt and Fairouz Kamareddine

Texts in Computing Series Editor
Ian Mackie, King's College London

Programming Languages and Operational Semantics

An Introduction

Maribel Fernández

King's College London

ISBN 0-9543006-3-7
King's College Publications
Scientific Director: Dov Gabbay
Managing Director: Jane Spurr
Department of Computer Science
Strand, London WC2R 2LS, UK
kcp@dcs.kcl.ac.uk

Cover design by Richard Fraser, www.avalonarts.co.uk
Printed by Lightning Source, Milton Keynes, UK

Preface

Aim

The aim of this book is to present and compare alternative programming languages and paradigms. We explain the most significant constructs of modern imperative, functional and logic programming languages, and describe their operational semantics first in an informal way, and then using transition systems.

About This Book

This book provides a concise introduction to the essential concepts in programming languages, using operational semantics techniques. It is addressed to undergraduate students, as a complement to programming languages or operational semantics courses. Some sections are addressed to more advanced students, these are marked with (†). The book was actually developed to accompany lectures on programming language paradigms for a second year undergraduate course at King's College London. We assume that readers have good programming skills in one language; knowledge of more programming languages will be helpful but is not necessary.

Each chapter includes exercises which provide the opportunity to apply the concepts and techniques presented. Although some of the questions are just introductory, most exercises are designed with the goal of testing the *understanding* of the subject, for instance by requiring to adapt the techniques to different contexts. Some challenging exercises for more advanced students are also included, these are also marked with (†).

The book is organised as follows:

Chapter 1 gives an introduction to programming languages and operational semantics, and provides the background material for the rest of the book.

In Part I we study the main components of imperative languages. We first give an informal description in Chapter 2, and then give a formal specification of the main constructs in imperative languages using transition systems in Chapter 3.

Part II is dedicated to functional languages and their type systems. In Chapter 4 we give an overview of functional programming (using Haskell for our examples), and then give some examples of semantic descriptions of functional languages in Chapter 5.

Finally, in Part III we briefly study logic programming languages and describe the operational semantics of Prolog.

Although we have not included chapters on object-oriented languages specifically, we do study aspects of these languages in Chapters 1 and 2.

At the end of the book there is a bibliographical section with references to relevant articles and books where the interested reader can find more information. In particular, for each programming language there is a reference to its definition, which is indicated the first time the language is mentioned.

Acknowledgements

The material presented in this book has been prepared using several different sources, including the references mentioned above and previous versions of notes for my courses at King's College and in France. I would like to thank the reviewers, my colleagues, and the students of the Department of Computer Science at King's for their comments on previous versions of the book, and the editors of the Texts in Computing series at King's College Publications for inviting me to contribute to the series.

Maribel Fernández
King's College London

Contents

II   Functional Languages   55

III   Logic Languages   115

Chapter 1

Introduction

This book is concerned with programming languages.

Programming languages are tools for writing software; they enable the user to communicate with the computer. There are hundreds of programming languages in use in the world. Many of the languages that exist today have evolved from older languages, and are likely to continue evolving in the future. In order to understand these plethora of languages and adapt easily to changes in the languages we are familiar with, it is useful to study the concepts underlying programming languages in general. We will study the main components of programming languages, and some of the tools that are used to describe in a precise way the behaviour of their main constructs, in order to:

- understand the differences between apparently similar constructs in different languages;

- be able to choose a suitable programming language for each application;

- increase our ability to learn new languages and our ability to adapt to changes in existing languages;

- design new languages: the general concepts underlying programming language design can also be applied to the design of other kind of languages, for instance in user-interfaces for software applications.

1.1 Programming Languages and Software Engineering

Programming languages are used in several phases in the software development process: in the implementation phase obviously, but also in the design phase to describe the decomposition of the system into modules which later will be coded and tested.

There are various design methods in use, for example: top-down design, functional design, object-oriented design. Some languages provide better support for design methods than others:

- Older languages such as Fortran (the first version was reported in 1954 [5]) do not support any specific design method.

- More modern languages were designed to support a specific design method: for example, Pascal [22] supports top-down development and structured programming, Haskell [13] supports functional design, Java [3] supports object-oriented design and programming.

If the design method is not compatible with the programming language in which the application will be coded, the programming effort increases. When they are compatible, the design abstractions can easily be mapped into program components. For this reason the style of the programming language is often reflected in the design of the software application. For instance, we will probably tend to reason in terms of functions if we are going to use a functional language, or in terms of objects if we are going to use an object-oriented language.

1.2 Programming Paradigms

A programming language may induce a particular style of programming and a particular set of methods and techniques to reason about programs, called a *programming paradigm*. Programming languages are usually classified according to the paradigm they support. The main classes are:

- **Imperative Languages**: Programs are decomposed into *computation steps* (also called commands, statements, or instructions), reflecting the step-wise execution of programs in usual hardware. Subprograms (also called routines or procedures) are used to modularise the program. Programs written in imperative languages give accurate descriptions of *how* to solve a given problem. For example: Fortran, Algol [11], Pascal, and C [6] are imperative languages.

- **Functional Languages**: Programs are functions, which can be composed to build new functions as in the mathematical theory of functions (which is the basis of these languages). This class of languages is also called declarative, since the focus is in *what* should be computed, not *how* it should be computed. Functional languages emphasise the use of expressions which are evaluated by simplification. For example: Haskell, SML [10], Caml [20] and Clean [15] are functional languages.

- **Object-oriented Languages**: Programs are collections of objects which can only be accessed through the operations (or methods) defined on them, and which are hierarchically organised. For example: Java is an object-oriented language. Object-oriented design focuses on entities that combine data (fields) and operations (methods). The designer produces a hierarchical description of the structure of the system which is the basis for the implementation in an object-oriented language. Object-orientation is sometimes considered as a feature of imperative languages, however, it can also be found in functional languages and it can be combined with logic languages too. Therefore we see it as a paradigm of programming on its own right. However, this class of languages is out of the scope of this book.

- **Logic Languages**: Programs describe a problem rather than defining an algorithmic implementation. Again this class of languages is declarative, since the focus is in the specification of the problem that needs to be solved and not on how it is solved. A logic program is a description (using the language of first-order logic) of facts and properties about a problem. The most well-known logic programming language is Prolog [18], which was designed by Colmerauer, Roussel and Kowalski in the 70's. More modern logic programming languages combine logic programming and constraint-solving.

1.3   Components of a Programming Language

A programming language has three main components:

1. *Syntax:* defines the form of programs. It indicates how expressions, commands, declarations are built and put together to form a program.

2. *Semantics:* gives the *meaning* of programs. It indicates how programs behave when they are executed.

3. *Implementation:* a software system that can read a program and execute it in a machine (e.g. compiler or interpreter), plus a set of tools (editors, debuggers, etc).

We will describe each of these components, starting from implementation.

1.3.1   Language Implementation

Low-level languages are machine-dependent. For example, machine instructions, and even assembly languages in which names are given to machine instructions and data, are low-level languages. In this book we are concerned with high-level programming languages, which are (more or less) independent from the machine.

Machine independence is good in terms of portability of the code, but it means that the hardware of the computer is not able to execute the language commands directly. We therefore need special programs (consisting of machine instructions and running directly on hardware) which are able to read and execute our high-level programs. In order words, we need an implementation of the language.

High-level programming languages can be implemented by:

- *Compiling* programs into machine language,

- *Interpreting* programs,

- using a *Hybrid Method* which combines compilation and interpretation.

To understand how programming languages are implemented, we will first give a brief overview of computer architecture.

Computer Architecture

The main components of a *von Neumann machine* (the most popular kind of computer) are:

- Memory, which contains data and machine instructions represented as sequences of bits;

- Registers;

- Processor (also called Central Processing Unit, CPU), with a set of machine instructions for arithmetic and logic operations called *machine language*;

- Peripherals, which may include a keyboard, display, mouse, printer, etc;

- File Systems.

The *operating system* supplies higher-level primitives than those of the machine language (e.g. input/output operations, file management system, editors). For example: Linux, Unix, MS DOS are operating systems. Language implementations are built on top of these, and user programs form the top layer, as shown in the following diagram.

user programs

---

language implementation

---

operating system

---

hardware

The three layers including machine hardware, operating system and language implementation are sometimes called a *virtual machine*. This is because if we have an implementation of say, the language C, then by abstracting the intermediate levels we can think of the system as a machine that executes C instructions, i.e. a C machine.

Compilation

The compiler is a program which translates the *source language* (usually a high-level language) into *object language* (usually machine language). The output of the compiler is a program that can be executed directly on the computer, although sometimes another program is used (a *linker*) in order to include code from libraries into an executable binary program.

Once our original program has been compiled, we can run it by executing the binary program produced by the compiler (and possibly the linker). Of course we can run the program many times and supply different input data without having to repeat the compilation process.

This method of implementation of programming languages provides *fast program execution*, as usually compilers are optimised so that the machine code produced is very efficient.

The main phases of the compilation process are:

1. *Lexical Analysis.*

   The building blocks of a programming language are lexical units called *tokens.* For example, identifiers (such as names of variables), keywords (such as begin, if, then, else, etc), separators (such as comma, colon, semicolon) are tokens. The lexical analyser, which is sometimes called *lexer*, reads a file containing a program (that is, reads the sequence of characters that forms a program) and identifies a sequence of tokens which are then passed to the syntax analyser. The lexical analyser may also produce an error message, if the characters in the input do not correspond to any of the tokens of the language.

2. *Syntax Analysis (Parsing).*

   The syntax analyser, also called *parser*, reads a sequence of tokens and produces a parse tree (or syntax tree) for the program, or an error message if the sequence of tokens does not obey the rules of the language. In order to check that the sequence of tokens corresponds to a syntactically correct program, the parser uses a formal definition of the syntax of the language, usually given by a *grammar.*

3. *Type and Semantics Analysis.*

   Some programming languages are *typed* and at compile time programs are checked to detect type errors. Programs that do not respect the typing rules of the language are rejected by the compiler[1]. Usually the syntax tree is used for type checking, and also for (optional) code optimisations.

4. *Machine Code Generation.*

   The code generator produces a machine language program equivalent to the optimised syntax tree (and to the original source program).

To actually run the program, we need to execute the object code produced by the compiler (and possibly by the linker). The execution of machine code occurs in a process called *fetch-execute cycle.* Each machine instruction to be executed is moved from the memory, where the program is stored, to the processor. The fetch-execute cycle consists of:

- Initialise Program Counter (also called Instruction Pointer), in a register of the machine;

- Repeat:

---

[1]In some typed languages the compiler does not check types but introduces code so that types can be checked at run time.

- fetch the instruction pointed by the Program Counter;
- increment the Program Counter;
- decode and execute the instruction.

When all the instructions in the program have been executed the control returns to the operating system (of course, in a system where more than one program is running the process is more complex).

Interpretation

In this case there is no translation: an interpreter is a program which reads, analyses and directly executes the instructions of a high-level language (or produces an error message when a lexical, syntactic or semantic error is detected).

The interpreter simulates a machine whose fetch-execute cycle deals with high-level program instructions; in other words, the interpreter provides us with a *virtual machine* whose machine code is a high-level language.

The advantage of interpretation over compilation is that interpreters are easier to implement than compilers, and it is easier to debug programs in interpreted languages (interpreters provide better error messages). However, there is no optimisation of code and in general the execution of programs in interpreted languages is slower.

Simpler languages, and prototyping languages, are usually interpreted (for example: LISP and Unix Shell Scripts are interpreted).

Some languages have both an interpreted and a compiled version. The interpreter can be used for didactic purposes, to write prototype software applications, or to develop and debug programs which are later compiled to increase execution speed. For example, for the study of functional programming languages later in this book we will use an interpreter for Haskell (called Hugs) but compilers are also available (for example, ghc).

Hybrid Implementation

Some languages are implemented by translation (compilation) to an intermediate simpler language, instead of machine language. This intermediate language is then interpreted.

The advantage of this solution is portability: in this way programs can be executed in any machine that has an interpreter for the intermediate language.

There are many examples of this technique. Pascal was one of the first languages implemented in this way. Many functional languages are translated to abstract machine code which is interpreted. Also Java compilers produce an intermediate language (bytecode) and programs can then be executed in any machine with a bytecode interpreter.

1.3.2 Syntax

The *syntax* of a programming language is concerned with the *form* of programs. It specifies the set of characters that can be used to write programs, and provides rules indicating how to form lexical units and how to combine them to build expressions, commands, etc.

We have to distinguish between *concrete syntax* and *abstract syntax* of programming languages. The concrete syntax describes which chains of characters are well-formed programs, whereas the abstract syntax describes the syntax trees, to which a semantics is associated. In other words, the concrete syntax describes the actual programs, whereas the abstract syntax describes their representation (the output of the syntax analyser). Below we give an example, using arithmetic expressions. First we need to introduce some terminology.

Formally, a language is a set of *words* built out of characters. To specify the syntax of programming languages we use *grammars*. A grammar can be used to generate the words of a language, or to check that a given word belongs to a given language. It is specified by:

- an alphabet: a set of symbols containing all the characters, or *terminals*, of the language, plus additional *non-terminal* symbols used to generate the words;

- a set of rules which indicate how words are built; and

- a distinguished non-terminal (called *initial symbol*) which is used as a starting point for the generation of words.

Sometimes the alphabet is not explicitly given, since it can be deduced from the rules of the grammar. The initial symbol is usually assumed to be the left-hand side of the first rule.

Example 1 (Arithmetic Expressions) *The concrete syntax of arithmetic expressions can be defined by the following grammar, where the alphabet contains the terminals* $0, 1, 2, 3, 4, 5, 6, 7, 8, 9, +, -, *, div$, *and the nonterminals* $Exp, Num, Op, Digit$. Exp *is the initial symbol. The rules to form expressions are:*

$$
\begin{array}{lll}
Exp & ::= & Num \mid Exp\,Op\,Exp \\
Op & ::= & + \mid - \mid * \mid div \\
Num & ::= & Digit \mid Digit\,Num \\
Digit & ::= & 0 \mid 1 \mid 2 \mid 3 \mid 4 \mid 5 \mid 6 \mid 7 \mid 8 \mid 9
\end{array}
$$

In this example we are using an extended Backus Naur Form (BNF), where the symbol | in the right hand side of a rule is understood as an "or". For instance, the first rule indicates that an expression is a number or it is formed by an expression followed by an operator, followed by another expression.

To build an expression, we start with the non-terminal Exp and use the rules from left to right, until we obtain a word containing only terminals.

For instance, we can generate the expression $2 * 3 + 4$ as follows:

$$
\begin{array}{llll}
Exp & \to & Exp\,Op\,Exp & \to & Num\,Op\,Exp \\
& \to & Digit\,Op\,Exp & \to & 2\,Op\,Exp \\
& \to & 2 * Exp & \to & 2 * Exp\,Op\,Exp \\
& \to & 2 * Num\,Op\,Exp & \to & 2 * Digit\,Op\,Exp \\
& \to & 2 * 3\,Op\,Exp & \to & 2 * 3 + Exp \\
& \to & 2 * 3 + Num & \to & 2 * 3 + Digit \\
& \to & 2 * 3 + 4
\end{array}
$$

The problem with this definition of arithmetic expressions is that there are several ways of deriving an expression, which causes ambiguity (because the syntax tree associated to the expression depends on the derivation). In particular, the expression $2 * 3 + 4$ above can also be derived as:

$$
\begin{array}{llll}
Exp & \to & Exp\,Op\,Exp & \to & Exp\,Op\,Num \\
& \to & Exp\,Op\,Digit & \to & Exp\,Op\,4 \\
& \to & Exp + 4 & \to & Exp\,Op\,Exp + 4 \\
& \to & Exp\,Op\,Num + 4 & \to & Exp\,Op\,Digit + 4 \\
& \to & Exp\,Op\,3 + 4 & \to & Exp * 3 + 4 \\
& \to & Num * 3 + 4 & \to & Digit * 3 + 4 \\
& \to & 2 * 3 + 4
\end{array}
$$

The first derivation will produce a syntax tree corresponding to $2 * (3+4)$, whereas the second gives $(2 * 3) + 4$, with a different result.

The following grammar describes the abstract syntax of arithmetic expressions: n represents numbers (seen as terminals); e and op are non-terminals.

$$
\begin{array}{lll}
e & ::= & n \mid op(e, e) \\
op & ::= & + \mid - \mid * \mid div
\end{array}
$$

Note that this grammar defines syntax trees where the leaves are numbers and internal nodes are labelled with operators. Since it specifies trees, there are no ambiguities.

In the rest of the book we will only work with the abstract syntax of programming languages. This is because we are interested in the *semantics* of the various constructs of programming languages. The concrete syntax is not relevant from a semantics point of view, although of course when writing a program it is important to know the concrete syntax of the language, as programs that do not respect the constraints will be rejected by the compiler or the interpreter.

1.3.3   Semantics

The *semantics* of a language defines the meaning of programs, that is, how they behave when they are executed on a computer.

Similar constructs are often used in different languages with different syntax and different semantics. Variations in concrete syntax are in general superficial, but differences in meaning are important since apparently similar constructs may produce very dissimilar results.

The semantics of a programming language can be defined at two levels: *static semantics* or *typing*, and *dynamic semantics*, or just semantics. We will briefly describe both.

Static Semantics

Types can be seen as specifications of programs, and therefore they are part of the semantics of the language, but they are a form of static semantics. The goal is to detect (before the actual execution of the program) programs that are syntactically correct but will give errors during execution.

Example 2 *Consider a language with arithmetic and boolean expressions where the abstract syntax is given by:*

$$e \quad ::= \quad n \mid b \mid op(e, e)$$
$$op \quad ::= \quad + \mid - \mid * \mid div \mid nand \mid nor$$

n represents numbers and b booleans. The expression $+(1, True)$ is syntactically correct, but it is not typeable: attempting to add a number and a boolean should produce a type error.

Most typed languages require type declarations associating types with program constructs. In some functional languages, types can be *infered*, which frees the programmer from the need of writing type declarations. We will study type checking and type inference systems in Chapters 4 and 5.

Dynamic Semantics

The dynamic semantics of the language describes the behaviour of programs at execution time. It is often given by informal definitions and explanations in natural language (e.g. English) in language manuals, which are in general imprecise and incomplete. A few languages have a formal semantics.

Formal semantics are useful in various contexts, for several reasons:

1. Language Implementation: A formal definition of the semantics of the language facilitates its implementation. This is because the semantics specifies the behaviour of each construct in abstract terms, providing a description of the execution process which is independent of the actual machine. Compilers and interpreters are ultimately software applications, and as for any software application, it is easier to write it if we have a clear and complete specification of what it should do.

2. Programming: Programmers obviously benefit from a clear description of the constructs in the language. Moreover formal semantics usually provide tools or techniques to reason about programs and to prove properties of programs.

3. Language Design: A formal semantics prevents ambiguities in the constructs, and suggests improvements and new constructs. For example, the study of the λ-calculus as a model of computation has influenced the design of functional and object-oriented languages.

However, formal semantics descriptions can be hard to produce and difficult to read, so usually only a part of the language is formally defined.

There are different approaches to the formal definition of the semantics of programming languages. The main semantic styles are:

- *Denotational:* The meaning of expressions, and in general, the meaning of the constructs in the language, is given in an abstract way using a mathematical model for the language. The semantics describes the *effect* of each construct.

- *Axiomatic:* The meaning of programs is given by describing the properties that hold before and after the execution of the program, using axioms and deduction rules in a specific logic. For each kind of construct, predicates or assertions are given, describing the constraints on program variables before and after the execution of the statement. These are called *precondition* and *postcondition*.

- *Operational:* The meaning of each construct is given in terms of computation steps. *Transition systems* are used as a tool to give the operational semantics of programs: the execution of the program is described as a sequence of transitions. Transition systems can be presented as abstract machines where the transitions represent changes of state in the machine, or using axioms and rules to define a transition relation (structural operational semantics).

Each style of semantics has its advantages, they are complementary. Operational semantics is very useful for the implementation of the language and for proving correctness of compiler optimisations, since it describes the computation steps that are required to execute each command. On the other hand, denotational semantics and axiomatic semantics are useful to reason about programs and to prove properties of programs.

In this book we will only study operational semantics of programming languages, using transition systems. In the rest of this chapter we give the necessary mathematical background.

1.4 Mathematical Background

1.4.1 Transition Systems

A transition system is a mathematical device that can be used to model computation.

Definition 3 (Transition System) *A transition system is specified by*

- *A set Config of configurations or states,*

- *A binary relation $\rightarrow \subseteq$ Config $\times$ Config, called transition relation.*

  We use the notation $c \rightarrow c'$ (infix) to indicate that c, c' are related by $\rightarrow$.

The expression $c \rightarrow c'$ denotes a *transition* from c to c'. A transition can be understood simply as a change of state.

We denote by $\rightarrow^*$ the reflexive transitive closure of the relation $\rightarrow$. Therefore $\rightarrow^*$ is a binary relation that contains $\rightarrow$, contains all the pairs $c \rightarrow^* c$ (reflexivity), and all the pairs $c \rightarrow^* c'$ such that $c \rightarrow^* c''$ and $c'' \rightarrow^* c'$ for some c'' (transitivity). In other words, $c \rightarrow^* c'$ holds if and only if there is a sequence of transitions:

$$c \rightarrow c_1 \rightarrow \ldots \rightarrow c_n = c' \qquad \text{where } n \geq 0.$$

We will distinguish *initial* and *final* (also called *terminal*) subsets of configurations, written I, T respectively. A final configuration c is characterised by the fact that there is no transition out of c, more precisely: for all $c \in T$ there is no c' such that $c \rightarrow c'$.

The intuitive idea is that a sequence of transitions from an initial state $i \in I$ to a final state $t \in T$ represents a run of the system.

Definition 4 *A transition system is* deterministic *if for every configuration c, whenever* $c \to c_1$ *and* $c \to c_2$ *we have* $c_1 = c_2$.

In a deterministic system, at each point of the computation there is at most one possible transition.

Historically, transition systems were the first tool used to give formal semantics of a programming language. The first formal description of the behaviour of a program was in terms of an abstract machine.

Definition 5 *An* abstract machine *for a programming language is a transition system that simulates the execution of programs, more precisely, it specifies an interpreter for a programming language.*

In Chapter 3 we will give an example abstract machine for a simple imperative language.

Abstract machines are very useful for implementing a programming language since they describe the execution of each command step by step. However, for users of the language they are not always easy to understand because there are too many details. For this reason, abstract machines are also difficult to use to reason about programs, or to prove properties of programs.

It is possible to specify the operational semantics of the language in a more structured way, abstracting some of the implementation details. The structural approach to operational semantics based on transition systems gives an *inductive* definition of the execution of a program. The transition relation is defined by induction, and each command is described in terms of its components. We will give examples of structural operational semantics for imperative and functional languages, in Chapters 3 and 5.

1.4.2 Induction

Let $\mathcal{N}$ be the set of natural numbers: $\{0, 1, 2, 3, \ldots\}$. The Principle of Mathematical Induction says that to prove that a certain property P holds for all the natural numbers, which we write as

$$\forall n \in \mathcal{N}.P(n)$$

it is sufficient to show:

- *Basis:* $P(0)$.

- *Induction Step:* $P(n)$ implies $P(n + 1)$ for every natural number n; this is written:
$$\forall n \in \mathcal{N}.(P(n) \Rightarrow P(n + 1))$$

The assumption $P(n)$ in the induction step is called Induction Hypothesis.

Example 6 *We use the notation*

$$\sum_{i=1}^{n} expression_i$$

to represent the sum of $expression_1, \ldots, expression_n$. *For instance,*

$$\sum_{i=1}^{n} i = 1 + \ldots + n$$

We can prove by induction that

$$\sum_{i=1}^{n} (2i - 1) = n^2$$

for all natural numbers n *as follows:*
   Basis: $0 = 0^2$
   Induction Step: Assume $\sum_{i=1}^{n} (2i - 1) = n^2$, *then*

$$\sum_{i=1}^{n+1} (2i - 1) = \sum_{i=1}^{n} (2i - 1) + 2(n + 1) - 1 = n^2 + 2n + 1 = (n + 1)^2.$$

Induction on Lists.   We can adapt the induction principle to more general data structures, for instance lists. Assume we denote an empty list by *nil*, and a non-empty list by *cons(h, l)* where h is the head element and l is the tail of the list. We can define operations on lists by induction. For example, it is natural to define the length of a list by cases:

- *length(nil) = 0,*

- *length(cons(h, l)) = length(l) + 1.*

In the same way, we can give an induction principle for lists as follows:
   To prove that a property P holds for every list, it is sufficient to prove:

- *Basis: P(nil),*

- *Induction Step: P(l) implies P(cons(h, l)) for each element h and list l.*

   Here the assumption $P(l)$ is the Induction Hypothesis.

Example 7 *The mirror image of a list, which we call its* reverse, *is inductively defined as follows:*

- *reverse(nil) = nil,*

- *reverse(cons(h, l)) = append(reverse(l), h), where the append operation simply adds the element h at the end of the list reverse(l).*

We show by induction that for any list, its mirror image is a list of the same length.

- *Basis: The reverse of nil is also nil, so the property holds trivially in this case.*

- *Induction Step: Given a non-empty list cons(h, l), we remark that by the induction hypothesis l and its reverse have the same length n, and both the original list cons(h, l) and its reverse have one additional element. Therefore they both have length n + 1.*

Structural Induction. The induction principle for lists is a particular case of the Structural Induction Principle, which applies to finite labelled trees.

To prove a property P for finite labelled trees, it is sufficient to show:

- *Basis:*

  $P(l)$, for all leaf nodes l

- *Induction Step:*

  For each tree constructor c (with $n \geq 1$ arguments), if the property holds for any trees $t_1, \ldots, t_n$ then it holds for $c(t_1, \ldots, t_n)$. More precisely:

  $$\forall c, t_1, \ldots, t_n.(P(t_1) \wedge \ldots \wedge P(t_n) \Rightarrow P(c(t_1, \ldots, t_n)))$$

  In the induction step, $P(t_1), \ldots, P(t_n)$ are the induction hypotheses.

Example 8 *To prove that a property P holds for all abstract syntax trees corresponding to integer expressions as defined in Example 1 (that is, expressions built out of natural numbers and binary operators +, *, −, div), we proceed as follows:*

1. *Basis: Prove P(n) for all numbers n.*

2. *Induction Step: For all integer expressions E, E' and operators $op \in \{+, *, -, div\}$: prove that $P(E)$ and $P(E')$ implies $P(op(E, E'))$.*

The principle of structural induction can be justified by the principle of mathematical induction. This is because we work with *finite* trees, so we can understand structural induction as induction on the *size* of the tree.

More precisely: Let $P'(n)$ be the property:

for each finite labelled tree t of size at most n, $P(t)$ holds.

Then, $\forall t.P(t)$ is equivalent to $\forall n.P'(n)$.

Inductive Definitions. In addition to using induction to prove properties, we will use it also to define subsets of a given set T. We will write inductive definitions using *axioms* (representing the basis) and *rules* (representing the induction step).

Definition 9 (Axioms and Rules) *An axiom is simply an element of T. A rule is a pair (H, c) where*

- *H is a non-empty subset of T, called the* hypotheses *of the rule*

- *c is an element of T, called the* conclusion *of the rule.*

Definition 10 (Inductive Set) *The subset I of T inductively defined by a collection A of axioms and R of rules consists of those $t \in T$ such that*

- *$t \in A$, or*

- *there are $t_1, \ldots, t_n \in I$ and a rule $(H, c) \in R$ such that $H = \{t_1, \ldots, t_n\}$ and $t = c$.*

To show that an element t of T is in the inductive set I it is sufficient to show that t is an axiom, or that there is a *proof tree* with root (conclusion) t where the leaves are axioms and for each non-leaf node t_i there is a rule $(\{t_{i1}, \ldots, t_{im_i}\}, t_i)$ relating t_i and its descendants $t_{i1}, \ldots, t_{im_i}$ in the tree. This kind of proof tree is usually written:

$$
\cfrac{\cfrac{\vdots \quad \cdots \quad \vdots}{t_{11} \quad \cdots \quad t_{1m_1}} \quad \cdots \quad \cfrac{\vdots \quad \cdots \quad \vdots}{t_{n1} \quad \cdots \quad t_{nm_n}}}{\cfrac{t_1 \quad \cdots \quad t_n}{t}}
$$

Example 11 (Inductive Definition of Evaluation) *We can define using axioms and rules an evaluation relation for the (abstract syntax trees of) integer expressions defined in Example 1. We will write $E \Downarrow n$ to indicate that the expression E evaluates to the number n.*

Axioms.
   A number is already a value. Therefore for each number we need an axiom: $0 \Downarrow 0$, $1 \Downarrow 1$, $2 \Downarrow 2$, etc. Instead of writing these explicitly, we will use an axiom scheme:

$$n \Downarrow n$$

which represents the infinite set of axioms obtained by replacing n with a number.
   In the sequel, we will not distinguish between axioms and axiom schemes. We will simply write $n \Downarrow n$, with the assumption that n is any number.

Rules.
   Similarly, we will need rules for each operator $op \in \{+, *, -, div\}$, which we represent as rule schemes:

$$\frac{E_1 \Downarrow n_1 \quad E_2 \Downarrow n_2}{op(E_1, E_2) \Downarrow n} \quad if\ n = (n_1\ op\ n_2)$$

In the sequel, rule schemes will simply be called rules since there is no ambiguity.

Rule Induction. Associated to inductive definitions using axioms and rules, there is a principle of induction, called Rule Induction.
   Let I be a set defined by induction with axioms and rules (A, R). To show that $P(i)$ holds for all i in I, it is sufficient to prove:

- *Basis:* $\forall a \in A.P(a)$

- *Induction Step:*
  $\forall(\{h_1, \ldots h_n\}, c) \in R.\ P(h_1) \wedge \ldots \wedge P(h_n) \Rightarrow P(c)$.

Example 12 *We can prove using rule induction that each arithmetic expression has a unique value under the evaluation relation given in Example 11. In other words, the relation $\Downarrow$ is a total function.*
   Basis: The basis of the induction holds trivially, since numbers have unique values.

Induction Step: For non-atomic expressions, we remark that the value of an arithmetic expression is uniquely determined by the values of its arguments, which are unique by the induction hypotheses.

Special Principle of Rule Induction.   In some cases we are only interested in proving a property for a subset J of the inductive set I defined by (A, R). We can then use a special case of the principle of rule induction, which says that to prove that a property $Q(x)$ holds for all the elements of J, it is sufficient to show:

- *Basis:* $\forall a \in (A \cap J).Q(a)$

- *Induction Step:* for all $(H, c) \in R$ such that $c \in J$,

$$(\forall h \in H \cap J.Q(h)) \Rightarrow Q(c).$$

1.5   Exercises

1. Using the grammar specifying the concrete syntax for arithmetic expressions in Example 1, show that $1 - 2 - 3$ is a valid expression but -2 is not. Indicate possible syntax trees for $1 - 2 - 3$ and associated results assuming that the arithmetic operators have the usual semantics.

2. Using the grammar specifying the abstract syntax for arithmetic expressions in Example 1, show that both $-(-(1,2),3)$ and $-(1,-(2,3))$ are valid. Which are their results (assuming that the arithmetic operators have the usual semantics)?

   Explain why $-(1,2,3)$ is not valid.

3. Modify the previous grammar to add a unary minus operator.

4. Assume we want to design a language L in which variable identifiers must be a sequence of letters or numbers starting with a capital letter. Give a grammar for identifiers in L.

5. Prove by mathematical induction:

$$\sum_{i=1}^{n} i = n(n + 1)/2$$

6. Prove that the principle of structural induction is correct by showing that it corresponds to a particular application of the principle of mathematical induction.

7. Give an inductive definition of the set of natural numbers using axioms and rules. Prove using rule induction:

$$\sum_{i=1}^{n} i = n(n+1)/2$$

8. (†) Show that the special principle of rule induction is a particular instance of the principle of rule induction. Hint: Given a set I defined by axioms and rules and a subset J of I, instead of proving $\forall x \in J.Q(x)$, we can prove $\forall x \in I.P(x)$ where $P(x)$ is the property $(x \in J \Rightarrow Q(x))$.

Part I

Imperative Languages

Chapter 2

General Features of Imperative Languages

Imperative languages are abstractions of the underlying von Neumann machine, in the sense that they retain the essential parts but drop out complicating, superfluous details. Low-level languages provide a very limited level of abstraction, whereas a high-level language can be seen as a virtual machine where, in general, memory manipulation is transparent for the programmer and input/output primitives are hardware independent.

The memory is one of the main components of the computer, storing instructions and data. Another important component is the processor. These are abstracted in a high-level imperative language by: variables, representing memory space, together with assignment instructions that modify their contents, and control structures that indicate the order of execution of instructions in the processor.

In order to understand the behaviour of programs in imperative languages we need to know the *properties of variables* and the *flow of control among instructions*.

2.1 Variables

A variable is characterised by its properties or attributes:

- *Name:* usually a string of characters with some constraints (for instance, a maximal length).

- *Type:* indicates the range of values that can be assigned to the variable, as well as the operations that are available. Some languages are untyped (for example, assembly languages). Many high-level languages have *static typing*, which means that types are associated to variables at compile time (either when a type declaration is processed or by using a type inference algorithm if there are no type declarations, as in ML). In languages with *dynamic typing*, such as LISP [8], types are associated to variables when values are assigned at run time. This provides some flexibility, but makes it impossible to type check programs at compile time and for this reason less errors can be detected before the execution. Moreover the code introduced to do the type checking at run time in dynamically typed languages introduces overheads.

- *Address:* the memory location to which the variable is associated (also called *left-value* or *l-value*, since it is required when the variable occurs at the left-hand side of an assignment instruction).

  The association between addresses and names is not simple: the same name may be associated to different addresses in different parts of the program, and in some languages it is possible to associate more than one name to the same address (e.g. using variant records in Pascal, or the EQUIVALENCE statement in Fortran).

- *Value:* the contents of the memory location associated to the variable (also called *right-value* or *r-value* since it is required when the variable occurs in the right-hand side of an assignment instruction).

- *Lifetime:* the time during which the variable is allocated to a specific memory location (between *allocation* and *deallocation*). Allocation is the process of assigning free memory space to variables. Deallocation occurs when the space used for the variable is placed back in the pool of available memory. We distinguish four classes of variables:

  1. *Static Variables* are bound to a memory location before the execution of the program begins, and remain bound until the end of the execution.

     The advantage of this kind of allocation is efficiency, since all addressing can be resolved at compile time and there is no allocation/deallocation at run time.

     The disadvantage is that with static variables storage cannot be reused, and we need to know in advance the number of memory cells that are required, which is not always possible (for instance, local variables in recursive programs cannot be static).

2. *Stack Dynamic Variables* are allocated to a memory location when the declaration of the variable is processed at run time. For example, local variables of recursive procedures are typically stack dynamic variables.

3. *Explicit Heap Dynamic Variables* are nameless variables that are allocated and deallocated by program instructions, using pointers. For example, in C++

```
int *intnode;
...
intnode = new int; /*allocates memory space for an
                                     int variable*/
...
delete intnode; /*deallocates the memory space to
                          which intnode points*/
```

In some languages only the allocation is done explicitly by program instructions, and the deallocation is implicit. For example, in Java objects are explicit heap dynamic, and are accessed through reference variables, but there is no way to destroy them explicitly: implicit garbage collection is used.

4. *Implicit Heap Dynamic Variables* are bound to storage only when they are assigned values, and their attributes may change when their values change. Examples of this kind of variable are strings and arrays in Perl and JavaScript.

The advantage is that this kind of variable provides flexibility in the use of the memory space, but the disadvantage is cost (in execution time) since all the attributes of the variable may vary during the execution (including type, array ranges, etc). This also makes error detection more difficult.

- *Scope:* the range of instructions in which the variable is visible (i.e. can be used). Variables can be classified as *local* or *global* depending on their scope. Local variables are those declared in the block of program that is executed. The variables that are visible but are not local are called global.

Some languages have static scoping rules whereas others have dynamic scoping:

– *Static Scope* means that the scope of each variable can be determined before the execution of the program (i.e. at compile time). When a variable is referenced, the compiler looks for its declaration in the same block and if there is no declaration then it looks in the parent block, and continues in this way until it reaches the main program. If no declaration is found then an error is detected.

For example, the following Pascal program contains several references to the variable x.

```
program main;
    var x : real;

    procedure P1;
        var x : integer;              { local variable }

        begin

        ... x ...

        end;

    procedure P2;
        begin

        ... x ...                     { global variable }

        end;

    begin

    ... x ...

    end.
```

Since Pascal has static scoping, the reference to x in P1 corresponds to the local integer variable, whereas the references to x in P2 and in the main program correspond to the global real variable.

– *Dynamic Scope* means that the scope of a variable depends on the calling sequence of subprograms instead of their declaration. In the previous example, if we assume dynamic scope, the reference to x in P2 may refer to the variable in P1 or in main depending on who called P2.

This implies that we cannot do static type checking (with the disadvantages that were already mentioned), and moreover programs are very difficult to understand. For this reason, dynamic scoping is not used in modern languages (it was used in the first versions of LISP).

2.2 Assignment

The assignment instruction is generally of the form:

$$variable\text{-}name = expression$$

but the = sign should not be confused with equivalence in the mathematical sense. To emphasise the difference, sometimes := is used instead of =.

This instruction associates to the variable named at the left the value of the expression indicated in the right, but only until a new value is stored with another assignment to the variable or by a side-effect of another instruction.

In typed languages, typing controls are performed (at compile time if the language has static typing) in order to ensure that the expression and the variable have compatible types.

The language C has a notation for combining assignment and increment: i++ and ++i change the value of i to the current value plus 1 and return the value of i and i+1 respectively. There are also instructions combining assignment and decrement, written --i and i--.

2.3 Control Statements

Programs in imperative languages are sequences of instructions. The sequencing is indicated by textual juxtaposition. The next instruction that will be executed is therefore the one that follows in the text of the program, unless a control statement is used.

The main control statements in imperative languages are:

- *selection constructs*, also called *conditionals*,

- *iterative constructs*, also called *loops*, and

- *branching instructions*.

Moreover, languages provide ways to build *compound control statements* by grouping together several instructions in *blocks*, for example using braces in C or Java.

It has been proved that any sequential algorithm can be coded with just two control statements: a selection construct (such as `if-then-else`) and a logically controlled iteration (such as `while`). Branching instructions (such as the controversial `go-to`) are therefore superfluous. However, all languages provide several constructs of each class, in order to facilitate the writing and reading of programs. For instance, most imperative languages include a `for` loop which is controlled by a counter.

2.3.1   Selection Statements

Selection constructs are used to choose between two or more execution paths in a program. We distinguish *two-way selectors* and *multiple selectors*.

- *Two-way selectors (if-then-else)* are standard in modern imperative languages. The concrete syntax varies depending on the language, the usual forms are:

  > `if` *condition* `then` *then-branch* `else` *else-branch*

  > or

  > `if` (*condition*) *then-branch* `else` *else-branch*

  These constructs cause the evaluation of the condition, and the selection of the *then-branch* if the condition is true, or the *else-branch* otherwise. Sometimes the `else` *else-branch* part is omitted and when the condition is false the next instruction in the program is executed.

  Although the semantics of a single selector is quite clear, the semantics of nested selectors varies depending on the language. For example, in a Java-like program:

  ```
  if (a == 0)
      if (b == 0)
      (result = 0)
  else
      (result = 1)
  ```

  is the `else` paired with the outer or inner `if`?

Most languages, including Java, specify that the else is matched with the most recent unpaired then clause (the inner one in the example above). Since this implicit association may be confusing, some languages require the use of specific syntax for nesting selectors. For example, in Algol 60, we write:

```
if a = 0 then
begin
    if b = 0 then
    result := 0
    else
    result := 1
end
```

or if we want to associate the else to the outer if, we write:

```
if a = 0 then
begin
    if b = 0 then
        result := 0
end
else
    result := 1
```

Note that to obtain the latter semantics in Java we also need to use extra syntax (braces).

- *Multiple selectors* are a generalisation of two-way selectors. The idea is that more than two alternative paths can be specified. Multiple selectors are usually associated to keywords such as case or switch.

  For example, in Java, C, or C++ we can write:

```
switch (expression) {
case expr-1 :  statement-1;
    ...
```

```
case expr-n :  statement-n;
[default :  statement-n+1]
}
```

In some languages (e.g. Pascal), at the end of a branch the control
goes to the instruction that follows the multiple selector, in others
(e.g. Java) we need an explicit break at the end of the branch in
order to go to the end of the switch (or a return to exit the method).

2.3.2   Iterative Statements (Loops)

Iterative constructs cause a statement or sequence of statements (the *body*
of the loop) to be repeated, until a certain condition holds.

If the test for loop completion is done before the execution of the body
we say that it is a *pre-test* loop, and if it occurs after the body is executed,
it is *post-test*.

In addition, we can distinguish two kinds of loops depending on the way
the repetition is controlled:

- *Counter-controlled loops:* The number of repetitions of the body of
  the loop depends on the value of a counter. For example, the for
  statement of C and Java:

```
for (expr-1; expr-2; expr3)
        loop-body
```

is executed as follows: expr-1 initialises the counter, expr-2 is the
loop control and is evaluated before each execution of the loop-body (it
is used to stop the loop), and expr-3 is evaluated after each execution
of the loop-body. For instance, the for instruction in the following
program

```
int sum;
int index;
sum = 0;
for (index = 0; index < 5; index++)
        sum = sum + list[index];
```

initialises the counter index in 0. The condition index < 5 is evaluated before each repetition of the assignment instruction, and index

is incremented after each repetition, until it is no longer smaller than 5.

In Java the control expression must be boolean, but C accepts also arithmetic expressions, in which case 0 is understood as False.

In other languages, the `for` instruction only indicates the name of the counter, and the range. For example, in Pascal we can write:

```
for index = 0 to 4 do
    sum := sum + list[index];
```

In this case the increment is 1, it is implicit (this is sometimes called the *step* of the for).

- *Logically-controlled loops:* Most imperative languages include both pre-test and post-test logically-controlled loop constructs. For example, in C++ and Java there is a `while` loop which has the form:

```
while (expression)
    loop-body
```

and a do loop, which has the form:

```
do
    loop-body
while (expression)
```

The `while` is pre-test, that is, the loop-body is executed as long as the expression evaluates to True. The `do` loop is post-test, therefore the loop-body is executed first and then the expression is evaluated, but in this case the loop-body is repeated until the expression evaluates to False.

There are other variants of logically-controlled loops. For example, in Pascal there is a post-test `repeat` loop which has the form:

```
repeat
    loop-body
until (expression)
```

This iterative construct executes the loop-body until the expression evaluates to True.

Finally, we remark that some languages, such as C, C++ and Java, allow the programmer to include in the loop-body statements that break the repetition (by exiting the loop body), but this makes programs more difficult to understand and reason about.

2.4 Structuring the Program: Blocks and Subprograms

A *block* is simply a group of statements, delimited by keywords such as begin and end, or by separators, like { and }. A block of statements is syntactically equivalent to one instruction, in other words, we can use a block in constructs where just one statement is expected. A block may contain not only commands but also declarations (of constants, variables or types). If the language has static scope, these will only be visible inside the block (they are local).

Subprogram is a generic name for a block that has a name and can be invoked explicitly. In this case the block of statements is executed upon invocation, and the control returns to the calling point after the execution of the subprogram. Typical examples are *procedures* in Pascal, *functions* in C, or *methods* in Java.

When a subprogram is declared, together with the name we can associate *parameters* or *arguments*, usually given between brackets after the name of the subprogram. These are called *formal parameters*, whereas the ones provided when the subprogram is called are the *actual parameters*. The values of the actual parameters will be replaced for the formal parameters when the subprogram is invoked. This can happen in several ways, and different languages use different *parameter passing mechanisms*. We will study these in more detail for functional languages, in Chapters 4 and 5.

2.5 Exercises

1. Some programming languages are untyped. What are the disadvantages of using a language without types? Is there any advantage?

2. What are the advantages of static variables in a programming language?

3. Define static scope and dynamic scope, and explain the differences. What are the advantages and disadvantages of dynamic scoping?

4. Consider the following Pascal program:

```
program main;
    var a : integer;
    procedure P1;
    begin
      writeln('a =', a)
    end;
    procedure P2;
    var a : integer;
    begin
      a := 10;
      P1
    end;
begin
a := 4;
P2
end.
```

Pascal uses static scoping rules. What is the value of a printed by P1? Under dynamic scoping rules, what would be the value printed?

5. Which kind of scoping rules (static or dynamic) does Java use?

   (a) Try to find the answer to this question in the documentation available for the language.

   (b) Write a test program and use its results to justify your answer to the previous question.

6. Some programming languages have a post-test logically controlled loop of the form:

$$\text{repeat } C \text{ until } B$$

where the loop-body C will be repeated until the boolean expression B evaluates to True.

Show that it is possible to simulate this kind of loop in a language that provides a pre-test loop such as:

$$\text{while } B \text{ do } C$$

Chapter 3

Operational Semantics of Imperative Languages

The discussion of programming language features in the previous chapter was informal. Informal semantics can be imprecise. Consider the following expression in C:

```
f(i++,--i)
```

What is its meaning? Depending on the order of evaluation of the parameters, the results are different. Actually, the order of evaluation of parameters of functions is not specified in the original definition of the language C, and therefore different C compilers could produce very different code for the same program.

To give a precise meaning to language constructs in use in imperative languages, in this chapter we will use a mathematical tool: transition systems.

The first approach to giving a precise, formal description of the behaviour of programming language constructs was in terms of an *abstract machine*. We recall that an abstract machine is a transition system that specifies an interpreter for the programming language. We will give an example for a small imperative language, which we call SIMP. Similar languages are described in [12, 14, 21].

3.1   Abstract Syntax of SIMP

Programs in SIMP can be commands (C), integer expressions (E), or boolean expressions (B):

$$P ::= C \mid E \mid B$$

Each syntactic category is defined below.

Commands.   As in every imperative language, in SIMP we have sequencing (indicated by the separator ;) and an assignment instruction. There is also a selector, a loop construct, and a skip instruction which will simply pass the control to the following statement.

$$C ::= \ skip \mid l := E \mid C; C \mid if \ B \ then \ C \ else \ C \mid while \ B \ do \ C$$

Integer Expressions.   We will only consider simple expressions, built out of numbers (denoted by n), variables (written $l, x, y, z, \ldots$) and arithmetic operators. To emphasise the fact that when a variable is used in an expression, it is the content of the memory location associated to the variable that is needed (its r-value), we write $!l$ instead of just l. The expression $!l$ denotes the value stored in l.

$$E ::= \ !l \mid n \mid E \ op \ E$$

$$op ::= \ + \mid - \mid * \mid /$$

In the rules above we assume that $n \in Z = \{\ldots, -2, -1, 0, 1, 2, \ldots\}$ (the set of integers) and $l \in L = \{l_0, l_1, \ldots\}$ (a set of *locations* or *variables*).

Boolean Expressions.   In the same way, we build boolean expressions using the boolean constants $True$ and $False$ (which we denote sometimes by b), boolean operators such as *and* ($\wedge$) and negation ($\neg$), and arithmetic comparisons involving integer expressions, such as $>, <, =$.

$$B ::= \ True \mid False \mid E \ bop \ E \mid \neg B \mid B \wedge B$$

$$bop ::= \ > \ \mid \ < \ \mid \ =$$

We now give some examples of programs in SIMP.

Example 13 *The following program swaps the contents of the variables x and y:*

$$z := !x \ ; \ x := !y \ ; \ y := !z$$

Assuming a natural number n is stored in the variable l, the following program computes its factorial $n!$ using the while command (which is the only iterative construct in SIMP*).*

> $factorial := 1;$
> $while \; !l > 0 \; do$
> $\qquad (factorial := !factorial *!l;$
> $\qquad l := !l - 1)$

Note that the grammar rules above specify the *abstract* syntax of SIMP, therefore the expressions should not be read as strings, but rather as labelled trees. The leaf nodes of the tree are labelled by elements of $Z \cup \{True, False\} \cup L \cup \{skip\}$ while the non-leaf nodes are labelled by operators and commands. We abuse notation by writing these 2-dimensional tree structures as strings. An example will help to clarify the notation.

Example 14 *The abstract syntax tree*

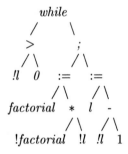

is written in a textual notation as:

$$while \; !l > 0 \; do \; (factorial := !factorial *!l; \; l := !l - 1)$$

using brackets where there is ambiguity.

Note that in Example 13, the program that swaps the contents of the variables x and y is ambiguous. To be precise, we should have written the brackets, either as

$$z := !x \; ; \; (x := !y \; ; \; y := !z)$$

or

$$(z := !x \; ; \; x := !y) \; ; \; y := !z$$

However, we will see later that both programs have exactly the same semantics (i.e. produce the same results).

3.2   An Abstract Machine for SIMP

To give the semantics of SIMP, we will define an abstract machine with

1. a *control stack* c, where instructions will be stored;

2. an *auxiliary stack* r, also called *results stack*, where intermediate results will be stored; and

3. a *memory*, also called *store*, modelled by a partial function m mapping locations to integers. We use the notation $dom(m)$ for the set of locations where m is defined, and write $m[l \mapsto n]$ to denote the function that associates to each $l' \neq l$ the value $m(l')$, and to l the value n.

The abstract machine is a transition system, and is therefore defined by a set of *configurations* and a set of *transition rules*.

Configurations. The configurations of the abstract machine for SIMP are triples $\langle c, r, m \rangle$ of control stack, results stack and memory. Stacks are inductively defined: an empty stack will be denoted by *nil*, and a non-empty stack $i \cdot c$ is obtained by pushing an instruction i on top of a stack c. The formal definition of the stacks c and r is given by the grammar:

$$c ::= nil \mid i \cdot c$$

$$i ::= P \mid op \mid \neg \mid \wedge \mid bop \mid := \mid if \mid while$$

$$r ::= nil \mid P \cdot r \mid l \cdot r$$

where P, *op* and *bop* are the non-terminals used in the rules defining the abstract syntax of SIMP in Section 3.1. In other words, the control stack may be empty, or contain programs, operators such as $+, -, *, /, >, <, =,$ $:=$, and keywords such as *if* or *while*. In the same way, the results stack may be empty or contain programs or locations.

To model the execution of SIMP programs we will define transitions between initial and final configurations.

Definition 15 (Initial Configurations) *To execute the command C in a given memory state m, the abstract machine will start from a configuration $\langle C \cdot nil, nil, m \rangle$. Configurations of this form will be called* initial.

Final configurations have the form $\langle nil, nil, m \rangle$, since the machine will stop when the stacks are empty.

Transition Rules. In Figure 3.1 we give a set of transition rules that generate a transition relation on configurations of the abstract machine. A transition

$$\langle c, r, m \rangle \to \langle c', r', m' \rangle$$

corresponds to a step of computation of the abstract machine, which will transform the configuration $\langle c, r, m \rangle$ into a new configuration $\langle c', r', m' \rangle$. The transition relation $\to$ specifies how to execute the instructions.

Definition 16 (Semantics of SIMP Commands) *If there is a sequence of transitions*

$$\langle C \cdot nil, nil, m \rangle \longrightarrow^* \langle nil, nil, m' \rangle$$

then we say that the program C executed in the state m terminates successfully producing the state m'.

The semantics of a command C in the state m *is described by giving the sequence of* transitions *that transform the configuration $\langle C \cdot nil, nil, m \rangle$ into $\langle nil, nil, m' \rangle$.*

Definition 17 (Semantics of SIMP Expressions) *If there is a sequence of transitions*

$$\langle E \cdot c, r, m \rangle \longrightarrow^* \langle c, v \cdot r, m' \rangle$$

or

$$\langle B \cdot c, r, m \rangle \longrightarrow^* \langle c, v \cdot r, m' \rangle$$

then we say that the value of the expression E (respectively B) in the state m is v.

We now give some examples of transitions of the abstract machine.

Example 18 *Let C be the program*

$$while\ B\ do\ C'$$

where B is the boolean expression $!l > 0$ and C' is the command

$$factorial := !factorial * !l;\ l := !l - 1$$

(see Example 13). Let m be the function that maps l to 4 and factorial to 1, which we denote as $\{l \mapsto 4, factorial \mapsto 1\}$.

1. Evaluation of Expressions:

$$\langle n \cdot c, r, m \rangle \;\; \rightarrow \;\; \langle c, n \cdot r, m \rangle$$
$$\langle b \cdot c, r, m \rangle \;\; \rightarrow \;\; \langle c, b \cdot r, m \rangle$$

$$\langle \neg B \cdot c, r, m \rangle \;\; \rightarrow \;\; \langle B \cdot \neg \cdot c, r, m \rangle$$
$$\langle (B_1 \wedge B_2) \cdot c, r, m \rangle \;\; \rightarrow \;\; \langle B_1 \cdot B_2 \cdot \wedge \cdot c, r, m \rangle$$
$$\langle \neg \cdot c, b \cdot r, m \rangle \;\; \rightarrow \;\; \langle c, b' \cdot r, m \rangle \qquad \text{if } b' = not\ b$$
$$\langle \wedge \cdot c, b_2 \cdot b_1 \cdot r, m \rangle \;\; \rightarrow \;\; \langle c, b \cdot r, m \rangle \qquad \text{if } b_1\ and\ b_2 = b$$

$$\langle (E_1\ op\ E_2) \cdot c, r, m \rangle \;\; \rightarrow \;\; \langle E_1 \cdot E_2 \cdot op \cdot c, r, m \rangle$$
$$\langle (E_1\ bop\ E_2) \cdot c, r, m \rangle \;\; \rightarrow \;\; \langle E_1 \cdot E_2 \cdot bop \cdot c, r, m \rangle$$
$$\langle op \cdot c, n_2 \cdot n_1 \cdot r, m \rangle \;\; \rightarrow \;\; \langle c, n \cdot r, m \rangle \qquad \text{if } n_1\ op\ n_2 = n$$
$$\langle bop \cdot c, n_2 \cdot n_1 \cdot r, m \rangle \;\; \rightarrow \;\; \langle c, b \cdot r, m \rangle \qquad \text{if } n_1\ bop\ n_2 = b$$

$$\langle !l \cdot c, r, m \rangle \;\; \rightarrow \;\; \langle c, n \cdot r, m \rangle \qquad \text{if } m(l) = n$$

2. Evaluation of Commands:

$$\langle skip \cdot c, r, m \rangle \;\; \rightarrow \;\; \langle c, r, m \rangle$$

$$\langle (l := E) \cdot c, r, m \rangle \;\; \rightarrow \;\; \langle E \cdot := \cdot c, l \cdot r, m \rangle$$
$$\langle := \cdot c, n \cdot l \cdot r, m \rangle \;\; \rightarrow \;\; \langle c, r, m[l \mapsto n] \rangle$$

$$\langle (C_1; C_2) \cdot c, r, m \rangle \;\; \rightarrow \;\; \langle C_1 \cdot C_2 \cdot c, r, m \rangle$$

$$\langle (if\ B\ then\ C_1\ else\ C_2) \cdot c, r, m \rangle \;\; \rightarrow \;\; \langle B \cdot if \cdot c, C_1 \cdot C_2 \cdot r, m \rangle$$
$$\langle (if \cdot c, True \cdot C_1 \cdot C_2 \cdot r, m \rangle \;\; \rightarrow \;\; \langle C_1 \cdot c, r, m \rangle$$
$$\langle (if \cdot c, False \cdot C_1 \cdot C_2 \cdot r, m \rangle \;\; \rightarrow \;\; \langle C_2 \cdot c, r, m \rangle$$

$$\langle (while\ B\ do\ C) \cdot c, r, m \rangle \;\; \rightarrow \;\; \langle B \cdot while \cdot c, B \cdot C \cdot r, m \rangle$$
$$\langle while \cdot c, True \cdot B \cdot C \cdot r, m \rangle \;\; \rightarrow \;\; \langle C \cdot (while\ B\ do\ C) \cdot c, r, m \rangle$$
$$\langle while \cdot c, False \cdot B \cdot C \cdot r, m \rangle \;\; \rightarrow \;\; \langle c, r, m \rangle$$

Figure 3.1: Transition Rules of the Abstract Machine for **SIMP**

Starting from the initial configuration $\langle C \cdot nil, nil, m \rangle$, the abstract machine will do the following transitions:

$$
\begin{aligned}
\langle C \cdot nil, nil, m \rangle \quad & \rightarrow \quad \langle B \cdot while \cdot nil, B \cdot C' \cdot nil, m \rangle \\
& \rightarrow \quad \langle !l \cdot 0 \cdot > \cdot while \cdot nil, B \cdot C' \cdot nil, m \rangle \\
& \rightarrow \quad \langle 0 \cdot > \cdot while \cdot nil, 4 \cdot B \cdot C' \cdot nil, m \rangle \\
& \rightarrow \quad \langle > \cdot while \cdot nil, 0 \cdot 4 \cdot B \cdot C' \cdot nil, m \rangle \\
& \rightarrow \quad \langle while \cdot nil, True \cdot B \cdot C' \cdot nil, m \rangle \\
& \rightarrow \quad \langle C' \cdot C \cdot nil, nil, m \rangle \\
& \rightarrow \quad \ldots \\
& \rightarrow \quad \langle nil, nil, m[l \mapsto 0, factorial \mapsto 24] \rangle
\end{aligned}
$$

The last configuration is a final one, therefore the sequence of transitions above gives the semantics of the program

> *while* !$l > 0$ *do*
> $\quad$ (*factorial* := !*factorial* ∗!l;
> $\quad l$:= !$l - 1$)

working in a memory where l contains the value 4 and factorial the value 1. It indicates that the program stops leaving the value 0 in l and 24 in factorial, as expected.

Note that not all the sequences of transitions are finite. For some initial configurations the machine may produce an infinite computation. If there is an infinite sequence of transitions out of $\langle C \cdot nil, r, m \rangle$, we say that the program C is *non-terminating* in the state m. For example, replacing the last command in the loop body of the program in the example above by l := !$l + 1$, we obtain a non-terminating program:

> *while* !$l > 0$ *do* (*factorial* := !*factorial* ∗ !l; l := !$l + 1$)

The abstract machine definition describes the exact behaviour of a while loop, in contrast with the informal definition: *"...the body of the loop is executed as long as the value of the expression is true. The test is done before the execution of the body..."* given in Chapter 2.

Another advantage of the abstract machine is that the transition rules explain the execution of the commands step by step, which is very useful if we have to implement the language. Since the semantics is precisely defined, it is possible to prove properties of programs. For example, to prove that a property P holds for all integer expressions in SIMP, we can use the Structural Induction Principle:

1. *Basis:* We have to consider numbers and basic expressions of the form
   $!l$. More precisely:

   - Prove $P(n)$ for all $n \in Z$
   - Prove $P(!l)$ for all locations l.

2. *Induction Step:*

   For all integer expressions E, E' and operators op:

   Prove that $P(E)$ and $P(E')$ implies $P(E\ op\ E')$.

Example 19 *We will prove that the semantics of* SIMP *guarantees that for any integer expression E occurring in a program working on a memory m, if E uses locations that are defined in m then the value of E is defined. In other words:*

For any configuration $\langle E \cdot c, r, m \rangle$ where c is any arbitrary control stack and r is also arbitrary, there is a configuration $\langle c, n \cdot r, m \rangle$ such that $\langle E \cdot c, r, m \rangle \to^* \langle c, n \cdot r, m \rangle$.

Formally, we have to prove $\forall E.P(E)$ where P is the property:

$$\forall m.locations(E) \in dom(m) \Rightarrow \exists n.\forall c.\forall r.\langle E \cdot c, r, m \rangle \to^* \langle c, n \cdot r, m \rangle$$

This is proved by induction on the structure of E:

- *Basis: If E is a number n or $!l$ then the transitions for constants and locations prove $P(E)$.*

- *Induction Step: Assume $P(E_1)$ and $P(E_2)$ hold, we prove $P(E_1\ op\ E_2)$ as follows.*

$$
\begin{aligned}
\langle (E_1\ op\ E_2) \cdot c, r, m \rangle \quad &\to \quad \langle E_1 \cdot E_2 \cdot op \cdot c, r, m \rangle \\
&\to^* \quad \langle E_2 \cdot op \cdot c, n_1 \cdot r, m \rangle \qquad by\ P(E_1) \\
&\to^* \quad \langle op \cdot c, n_2 \cdot n_1 \cdot r, m \rangle \qquad by\ P(E_2) \\
&\to^* \quad \langle c, n \cdot r, m \rangle \qquad where\ n = n_1\ op\ n_2.
\end{aligned}
$$

Although the abstract machine semantics is very useful for the implementation of the language, for users of the language (programmers) it is too detailed, and not always intuitive. Many transitions are doing just phrase analysis, only a few really perform computations. To overcome this problem another approach to operational semantics based on transition systems was developed: the *structural approach* due to Plotkin [16].

The idea is that transition systems should be structured in a way that reflects the structure of the language. The transitions for a compound statement should be defined in terms of the transitions for its substatements. In other words: the definition should be *inductive*.

For example, to describe the semantics of integer expressions in SIMP we can give an inductive definition of the evaluation process using axioms and rules, instead of sequences of transitions in the abstract machine. We write $(E, m) \Downarrow n$ to indicate that the expression E evaluates to n in the state m. The evaluation relation is defined by the axioms:

- $(n, m) \Downarrow n$ for all integer numbers n

- $(!l, m) \Downarrow n$ if $l \in dom(m)$ and $m(l) = n$

and rules of the form:

$$\frac{(E_1, m) \Downarrow n_1 \quad (E_2, m) \Downarrow n_2}{(E_1 \ op \ E_2, m) \Downarrow n} \quad \text{if } n = n_1 \ op \ n_2$$

3.3 Structural Operational Semantics for SIMP

In this section we define the structural operational semantics of SIMP as an alternative to the abstract machine. There are two styles of structural operational semantics:

- Small-step semantics, based on a *reduction* relation,

- Big-step semantics, based on an *evaluation* relation.

3.3.1 Reduction Semantics: Small-Step Semantics

The transition system defining the reduction semantics of SIMP is defined by:

- Configurations of the form
$$\langle P, s \rangle$$
where P is a SIMP program and s is a store represented by a partial function from locations to integers, as in the previous section. Recall that $s[l \mapsto n]$ denotes the function s' that coincides with s except that it associates to l the value n, more precisely:

$$s[l \mapsto n](l) = n \text{ and } s[l \mapsto n](l') = s(l') \text{ if } l \neq l'.$$

- A transition relation which is inductively defined by the axioms and rules shown in Figure 3.2. Note that there are axioms and rules for each syntactic construct, for this reason we say that the definition is *syntax directed*. However, there are some configurations to which no axiom or rule applies. For instance, configurations of the form:

  - $\langle n, s \rangle$ where n is an integer
  - $\langle b, s \rangle$ where b is a boolean
  - $\langle !l, s \rangle$ where $l \notin dom(s)$
  - $\langle skip, s \rangle$

which are *final*. In the case of $\langle !l, s \rangle$ where $l \notin dom(s)$ we say that the program is *blocked*.

We now give some examples of transitions.

Example 20 *Let P be the program $z := !x; (x := !y; y := !z)$ discussed in Examples 13 and 14, and assume the store s is such that $s(z) = 0$, $s(x) = 1$, $s(y) = 2$.*

Using the axioms and rules given in Figure 3.2, we can show that there is a sequence of transitions:

$$
\begin{aligned}
\langle P, s \rangle \quad &\rightarrow \quad \langle z := 1; (x := !y; y := !z), s \rangle \\
&\rightarrow \quad \langle skip; (x := !y; y := !z), s[z \mapsto 1] \rangle \\
&\rightarrow \quad \langle x := !y; y := !z, s[z \mapsto 1] \rangle \\
&\rightarrow \quad \langle x := 2; y := !z, s[z \mapsto 1] \rangle \\
&\rightarrow \quad \langle skip; y := !z, s[z \mapsto 1, x \mapsto 2] \rangle \\
&\rightarrow \quad \langle y := !z, s[z \mapsto 1, x \mapsto 2] \rangle \\
&\rightarrow \quad \langle y := 1, s[z \mapsto 1, x \mapsto 2] \rangle \\
&\rightarrow \quad \langle skip, s[z \mapsto 1, x \mapsto 2, y \mapsto 1] \rangle
\end{aligned}
$$

which proves that the program P is correctly swapping the contents of the variables x and y as specified.

In contrast with the abstract machine, each transition here is doing a part of the computation that leads to the result, whereas some of the transitions of the machine were only manipulating syntax. On the other hand, to see that a transition is valid we now need a proof. More precisely, since the transition relation is inductively defined with axioms and rules, to show that a pair $c \rightarrow c'$ is in the inductive set we have to show that it is an axiom or it is obtained by using a rule (see Definition 10 in Chapter 1). For example, to prove the validity of the first transition in the sequence above

$$
\langle z := !x; (x := !y; y := !z), s \rangle \rightarrow \langle z := 1; (x := !y; y := !z), s \rangle
$$

Reduction Semantics of Expressions:

$$\frac{}{\langle !l, s \rangle \rightarrow \langle n, s \rangle \;\; \text{if } s(l) = n} \; \text{(var)}$$

$$\frac{}{\langle n_1 \; op \; n_2, s \rangle \rightarrow \langle n, s \rangle \;\; \text{if } n = (n_1 \; op \; n_2)} \; \text{(op)}$$

$$\frac{}{\langle n_1 \; bop \; n_2, s \rangle \rightarrow \langle b, s \rangle \;\; \text{if } b = (n_1 \; bop \; n_2)} \; \text{(bop)}$$

$$\frac{\langle E_1, s \rangle \rightarrow \langle E_1', s' \rangle}{\langle E_1 op E_2, s \rangle \rightarrow \langle E_1' op E_2, s' \rangle} \; \text{(op}_\text{L}) \qquad \frac{\langle E_2, s \rangle \rightarrow \langle E_2', s' \rangle}{\langle E_1 op E_2, s \rangle \rightarrow \langle E_1 op E_2', s' \rangle} \; \text{(op}_\text{R})$$

$$\frac{\langle E_1, s \rangle \rightarrow \langle E_1', s' \rangle}{\langle E_1 bop E_2, s \rangle \rightarrow \langle E_1' bop E_2, s' \rangle} \; \text{(bop}_\text{L}) \qquad \frac{\langle E_2, s \rangle \rightarrow \langle E_2', s' \rangle}{\langle E_1 bop E_2, s \rangle \rightarrow \langle E_1 bop E_2', s' \rangle} \; \text{(bop}_\text{R})$$

$$\frac{}{\langle b_1 \wedge b_2, s \rangle \rightarrow \langle b, s \rangle \;\; \text{if } b = (b_1 \; and \; b_2)} \; \text{(and)}$$

$$\frac{}{\langle \neg b, s \rangle \rightarrow \langle b', s \rangle \;\; \text{if } b' = not \; b} \; \text{(not)} \qquad \frac{\langle B_1, s \rangle \rightarrow \langle B_1', s' \rangle}{\langle \neg B_1, s \rangle \rightarrow \langle \neg B_1', s' \rangle} \; \text{(notArg)}$$

$$\frac{\langle B_1, s \rangle \rightarrow \langle B_1', s' \rangle}{\langle B_1 \wedge B_2, s \rangle \rightarrow \langle B_1' \wedge B_2, s' \rangle} \; \text{(and}_\text{L}) \qquad \frac{\langle B_2, s \rangle \rightarrow \langle B_2', s' \rangle}{\langle B_1 \wedge B_2, s \rangle \rightarrow \langle B_1 \wedge B_2', s' \rangle} \; \text{(and}_\text{R})$$

Reduction Semantics of Commands:

$$\frac{\langle E, s \rangle \rightarrow \langle E', s' \rangle}{\langle l := E, s \rangle \rightarrow \langle l := E', s' \rangle} \; \text{(:=}_\text{R}) \qquad \frac{}{\langle l := n, s \rangle \rightarrow \langle skip, s[l \mapsto n] \rangle} \; \text{(:=)}$$

$$\frac{\langle C_1, s \rangle \rightarrow \langle C_1', s' \rangle}{\langle C_1; C_2, s \rangle \rightarrow \langle C_1'; C_2, s' \rangle} \; \text{(seq)} \qquad \frac{}{\langle skip; C, s \rangle \rightarrow \langle C, s \rangle} \; \text{(skip)}$$

$$\frac{\langle B, s \rangle \rightarrow \langle B', s' \rangle}{\langle if \, B \, then \, C_1 \, else \, C_2, s \rangle \rightarrow \langle if \, B' \, then \, C_1 \, else \, C_2, s' \rangle} \; \text{(if)}$$

$$\frac{}{\langle if \, True \, then \, C_1 \, else \, C_2, s \rangle \rightarrow \langle C_1, s \rangle} \; \text{(if}_\text{T})$$

$$\frac{}{\langle if \, False \, then \, C_1 \, else \, C_2, s \rangle \rightarrow \langle C_2, s \rangle} \; \text{(if}_\text{F})$$

$$\frac{}{\langle while \, B \, do \, C, s \rangle \rightarrow \langle if \, B \, then \, (C; while \, B \, do \, C) \, else \, skip, s \rangle} \; \text{(while)}$$

Figure 3.2: Axioms and Rules Defining Reduction for SIMP

when $s(z) = 0$, $s(x) = 1$, $s(y) = 2$, we use the axiom (var) and the rules (seq) and ($:=_R$) as follows:

$$\cfrac{\cfrac{\cfrac{}{\langle !x, s \rangle \to \langle 1, s \rangle} \text{ (var)}}{\langle z :=!x, s \rangle \to \langle z := 1, s \rangle} \text{ (:=}_R\text{)}}{\langle z :=!x; (x :=!y; y :=!z), s \rangle \to \langle z := 1; (x :=!y; y :=!z), s \rangle} \text{ (seq)}$$

The selection of the rules used in a proof is guided by the syntax of the program in the left-hand side configuration of the transition. The proof is obtained by traversing the abstract syntax tree of the program, and applying the rule or axiom that corresponds to the label of the root. In the program $z :=!x; (x :=!y; y :=!z)$ above, the root is a sequencing construct, therefore we first apply the rule (seq), with the hypothesis $\langle z :=!x, s \rangle \to \langle z := 1, s \rangle$. The latter can be proved using the rule ($:=_R$), which in turn requires the hypothesis $\langle !x, s \rangle \to \langle 1, s \rangle$. The latter is a particular case of the axiom (var), since $s(x) = 1$.

3.3.2   Evaluation Semantics: Big-Step Semantics

The transition system defining the reduction semantics of SIMP is *deterministic*: at each point, there is at most one possible transition. Therefore, given a configuration $\langle P, s \rangle$ there is a unique sequence of transitions starting from $\langle P, s \rangle$ and having maximal length. We can then associate to each program P in a state s an *evaluation* process, which corresponds to the longest sequence of transitions out of $\langle P, s \rangle$. This sequence may be finite or infinite. Infinite sequences correspond to *divergent* computations. Finite sequences can be classified according to the form of the last configuration. Recall that final configurations have the form $\langle n, s \rangle$ where n is an integer, $\langle b, s \rangle$ where b is a boolean, $\langle skip, s \rangle$, or are blocked configurations, such as $\langle !l, s \rangle$ where $l \notin dom(s)$.

Definition 21 (Evaluation) *The* evaluation sequence *for* $\langle P, s \rangle$ *is the uniquely defined sequence of transitions that starts with* $\langle P, s \rangle$ *and has maximal length. A* finite *evaluation sequence is called* terminating *if it eventually reaches a non-blocked configuration (such as* $\langle n, s \rangle$, $\langle b, s \rangle$ *or* $\langle skip, s \rangle$*), otherwise it is* blocked.

The evaluation relation *associates* $\langle P, s \rangle$ *with the* last *configuration of its evaluation sequence, provided the latter is finite. The usual notation for this is* $\langle P, s \rangle \Downarrow \langle P', s' \rangle$.

We now give examples of each class of evaluation sequence.

Example 22   *1. The configuration $\langle while\ True\ do\ skip, s\rangle$ is divergent, for any store s:*

> $\langle while\ True\ do\ skip, s\rangle \rightarrow$
> $\langle if\ True\ then\ (skip; while\ True\ do\ skip)\ else\ skip, s\rangle \rightarrow$
> $\langle skip; while\ True\ do\ skip, s\rangle \rightarrow$
> $\langle while\ True\ do\ skip, s\rangle \rightarrow$
> $\dots$

2. *If $dom(s)$ does not contain x, the configuration $\langle while\ !x > 0\ do\ C, s\rangle$ is blocked, no matter what the command C does:*

> $\langle while\ !x > 0\ do\ C, s\rangle \rightarrow$
> $\langle if\ !x > 0\ then\ (C; while\ !x > 0\ do\ C)\ else\ skip, s\rangle \nrightarrow$

There is no further transition since the rule (if) *requires a transition for $!x > 0$, which in turn requires the evaluation of $!x$ which is undefined.*

3. *For any store s, the configuration $\langle if\ 4 = 0\ then\ skip\ else\ skip, s\rangle$ is terminating:*

> $\langle if\ 4 = 0\ then\ skip\ else\ skip, s\rangle \quad \rightarrow$
> $\langle if\ False\ then\ skip\ else\ skip, s\rangle \quad \rightarrow$
> $\langle skip, s\rangle$

We will define a new transition system on configurations $\langle P, s\rangle$ such that the transition relation coincides with the evaluation relation.

The system of axioms and rules given in Figure 3.3 defines by induction the binary relation $\langle P, s\rangle \Downarrow \langle P', s'\rangle$ such that

$$\langle P, s\rangle \Downarrow \langle P', s'\rangle \text{ if } \langle P, s\rangle \rightarrow^* \langle P', s'\rangle \text{ where } \langle P', s'\rangle \text{ is final.}$$

Example 23 *Consider again a program P that swaps the contents of x and y:*

$$(z := !x; x := !y)\ ;\ y := !z$$

in a state s such that $s(z) = 0$, $s(x) = 1$, $s(y) = 2$.

We can show, using the axioms and rules given in Figure 3.3, that

$$\langle P, s\rangle \Downarrow \langle skip, s'\rangle$$

where $s'(z) = 1, s'(x) = 2, s'(y) = 1$.

$$\frac{}{\langle c, s \rangle \Downarrow \langle c, s \rangle \quad \text{if } c \in Z \cup \{True, False\}} \text{ (const)}$$

$$\frac{}{\langle !l, s \rangle \Downarrow \langle n, s \rangle \quad \text{if } s(l) = n} \text{ (var)}$$

$$\frac{\langle B_1, s \rangle \Downarrow \langle b_1, s' \rangle \quad \langle B_2, s' \rangle \Downarrow \langle b_2, s'' \rangle}{\langle B_1 \wedge B_2, s \rangle \Downarrow \langle b, s'' \rangle \quad \text{if } b = b_1 \text{ and } b_2} \text{ (and)}$$

$$\frac{\langle B_1, s \rangle \Downarrow \langle b_1, s' \rangle}{\langle \neg B_1, s \rangle \Downarrow \langle b, s' \rangle \quad \text{if } b = not\ b_1} \text{ (not)}$$

$$\frac{\langle E_1, s \rangle \Downarrow \langle n_1, s' \rangle \quad \langle E_2, s' \rangle \Downarrow \langle n_2, s'' \rangle}{\langle E_1\ op\ E_2, s \rangle \Downarrow \langle n, s'' \rangle \quad \text{if } n = n_1\ op\ n_2} \text{ (op)}$$

$$\frac{\langle E_1, s \rangle \Downarrow \langle n_1, s' \rangle \quad \langle E_2, s' \rangle \Downarrow \langle n_2, s'' \rangle}{\langle E_1\ bop\ E_2, s \rangle \Downarrow \langle b, s'' \rangle \quad \text{if } b = n_1\ bop\ n_2} \text{ (bop)}$$

$$\frac{}{\langle skip, s \rangle \Downarrow \langle skip, s \rangle} \text{ (skip)} \qquad \frac{\langle E, s \rangle \Downarrow \langle n, s' \rangle}{\langle l := E, s \rangle \Downarrow \langle skip, s'[l \mapsto n] \rangle} \text{ (:=)}$$

$$\frac{\langle C_1, s \rangle \Downarrow \langle skip, s' \rangle \quad \langle C_2, s' \rangle \Downarrow \langle skip, s'' \rangle}{\langle C_1; C_2, s \rangle \Downarrow \langle skip, s'' \rangle} \text{ (seq)}$$

$$\frac{\langle B, s \rangle \Downarrow \langle True, s' \rangle \quad \langle C_1, s' \rangle \Downarrow \langle skip, s'' \rangle}{\langle if\ B\ then\ C_1\ else\ C_2, s \rangle \Downarrow \langle skip, s'' \rangle} \text{ (if}_\mathsf{T})$$

$$\frac{\langle B, s \rangle \Downarrow \langle False, s' \rangle \quad \langle C_2, s' \rangle \Downarrow \langle skip, s'' \rangle}{\langle if\ B\ then\ C_1\ else\ C_2, s \rangle \Downarrow \langle skip, s'' \rangle} \text{ (if}_\mathsf{F})$$

$$\frac{\langle B, s \rangle \Downarrow \langle True, s_1 \rangle \quad \langle C, s_1 \rangle \Downarrow \langle skip, s_2 \rangle \quad \langle while\ B\ do\ C, s_2 \rangle \Downarrow \langle skip, s_3 \rangle}{\langle while\ B\ do\ C, s \rangle \Downarrow \langle skip, s_3 \rangle} \text{ (while}_\mathsf{T})$$

$$\frac{\langle B, s \rangle \Downarrow \langle False, s' \rangle}{\langle while\ B\ do\ C, s \rangle \Downarrow \langle skip, s' \rangle} \text{ (while}_\mathsf{F})$$

Figure 3.3: Axioms and Rules Defining Evaluation for SIMP

First notice that we can derive $\langle z :=!x, s \rangle \Downarrow \langle skip, s[z \mapsto 1] \rangle$:

$$\frac{\dfrac{}{\langle !x, s \rangle \Downarrow \langle 1, s \rangle} \text{ (var)}}{\langle z :=!x, s \rangle \Downarrow \langle skip, s[z \mapsto 1] \rangle} \text{ (:=)}$$

and also:

$$\frac{\dfrac{}{\langle !y, s[z \mapsto 1] \rangle \Downarrow \langle 2, s[z \mapsto 1] \rangle} \text{ (var)}}{\langle x :=!y, s[z \mapsto 1] \rangle \Downarrow \langle skip, s[z \mapsto 1, x \mapsto 2] \rangle} \text{ (:=)}$$

Therefore using the rule (seq) *we obtain:*

$$\langle z :=!x; x :=!y, s \rangle \Downarrow \langle skip, s[z \mapsto 1, x \mapsto 2] \rangle$$

We also have:

$$\frac{\dfrac{}{\langle !z, s[z \mapsto 1, x \mapsto 2] \rangle \Downarrow \langle 1, s[z \mapsto 1, x \mapsto 2] \rangle} \text{ (var)}}{\langle y :=!z, s[z \mapsto 1, x \mapsto 2] \rangle \Downarrow \langle skip, s[z \mapsto 1, x \mapsto 2, y \mapsto 1] \rangle} \text{ (:=)}$$

Hence we can derive $\langle P, s \rangle \Downarrow \langle skip, s' \rangle$ *using again* (seq).

We remark that, as for the small step semantics, the big step semantics is syntax-oriented. In order to obtain the proof for $\langle P, s \rangle \Downarrow \langle skip, s' \rangle$ in the example above, we use the rule (seq) twice since there are two sequencing operators in the program, and for each of the three assignment instructions in the program we use (:=) and (var).

3.4 Adding Blocks and Local Variables to SIMP (†)

We can add a notion of *local state* to SIMP by using blocks and local variable declarations. For this, we add to the syntax of SIMP a block constructor and local variable declarations and initialisations. We will use static scope rules, so that the scope of a newly created location corresponds precisely with the block where the location is created and initialised. The local variables will be either stack dynamic, in which case they will be allocated a memory space when the declaration is elaborated at run time and they will be deallocated at the end of the block, or explicit heap dynamic if they are declared as references, in which case their lifetime is not limited to the execution of the block.

Let us first define the (abstract) syntax of the new constructs.

Syntax.   We extend the grammar of SIMP, adding a new rule for commands:

$$C ::= begin \; loc \; l := E; \; C \; end$$

and a new rule for arithmetic expressions:

$$E ::= ref \; E$$

We use the keywords *begin* and *end* to indicate the limits of the block (as in Algol and Pascal). The idea is that the variable l will only be visible inside the block in which it is declared (i.e. it is a local variable), and it will be initialised with the value of the expression E, which in case we use references will be a pointer.

To give a precise meaning to these constructs, we add two rules to the big-step semantics.

Semantics.

$$\frac{\langle E, s \rangle \Downarrow \langle n, s' \rangle}{\langle ref \; E, s \rangle \Downarrow \langle l, s'[l \mapsto n] \rangle, \; if \; l \notin dom(s')} \text{(ref)}$$

The rule (ref) shows that the value of *ref E* is a new location, which has as contents the value of E.

$$\frac{\langle E, s \rangle \Downarrow \langle n, s' \rangle \quad \langle C\{z \mapsto l\}, s'[l \mapsto n] \rangle \Downarrow \langle skip, s''[l \mapsto n'] \rangle}{\langle begin \; loc \; z := E; C \; end, s \rangle \Downarrow \langle skip, s'' \rangle} \text{(loc)}$$

where

- $l \notin dom(s') \cup dom(s'') \cup locations(C)$, that is, l is a fresh name,

- $C\{z \mapsto l\}$ is the program C where all the occurrences of z are replaced by l.

The condition $l \notin dom(s') \cup dom(s'') \cup locations(C)$ ensures that when C is executed, the variable z is not confused with other variables with the same name in other parts of the program. We evaluate $C\{z \mapsto l\}$, that is, C where z has been replaced by the new variable l, in a store in which l has the value n (obtained by evaluating E). After the execution of the block the store is s'', where l has disappeared. The renaming of the local variable z by l guarantees that if there is another z in the program, its value is not affected by the execution of the block.

Example 24 *To see how the rule* (loc) *works, consider the program P that swaps the contents of x and y using a local variable z:*

> begin
>   loc $z := !x$;
> $x := !y$;
> $y := !z$
> end

We can show that the program P is correct as follows:
First we prove

$$\langle x := !y \, ; \, y := !l, s[l \mapsto s(x)]\rangle \Downarrow \langle skip, s[x \mapsto s(y), y \mapsto s(x)]\rangle$$

as in Example 23. Let us call s' the store $s[x \mapsto s(y), y \mapsto s(x)]$, then:

$$\frac{\dfrac{}{\langle !x, s\rangle \Downarrow \langle s(x), s\rangle} \text{ (var)} \qquad \langle x := !y \, ; \, y := !l, s[l \mapsto s(x)]\rangle \Downarrow \langle skip, s'\rangle}{\langle P, s\rangle \Downarrow \langle skip, s'\rangle} \text{ (loc)}$$

We can model procedure declarations and procedure calls in a similar way. SIMP could also be extended to include other looping constructs, or more powerful selectors such as a Java-style switch construct. However, this will not add more computational power to the language, and the semantic rules given in this chapter to describe the behaviour of while loops and conditionals can be easily adapted to model post-test loops and multiple selectors. We will not develop the operational semantics of imperative constructs further, instead in the following chapters we will study two classes of languages which are strikingly different from imperative languages in their use of variables and control structures: functional languages and logic programming languages.

3.5   Exercises

1. Draw the abstract syntax tree of the following SIMP programs:

    (a) $y := 0$;
       if $!x = !y$ *then* $(x := !x + 1; y := !y - 1)$
       else $(x := !x - 1; y := !y + 1)$

    (b) $C_1 ; (C_2 ; C_3)$ where C_1, C_2, C_3 are arbitrary programs.

    (c) $(C_1 ; C_2) ; C_3$ where C_1, C_2, C_3 are arbitrary programs.

2. Assume y has the value n for some natural number n. Write a program in SIMP to compute x^y.

3. Let C_1, C_2 and C_3 be arbitrary SIMP commands. Using the abstract machine semantics of SIMP, show that the programs $C_1; (C_2; C_3)$ and $(C_1; C_2); C_3$ have the same semantics (i.e. will give the same results when executed in the same state). Therefore the brackets are not needed.

4. Give another example of a program in SIMP for which there is an infinite sequence of transitions using the abstract machine semantics.

5. Give the structural induction principle for boolean expressions in SIMP.

6. (†) Explain why in the rules defining the small-step semantics of SIMP (Figure 3.2) there is no rule of the form:

$$\frac{\langle C_2, s \rangle \to \langle C'_2, s' \rangle}{\langle C_1; C_2, s \rangle \to \langle C_1; C'_2, s' \rangle}$$

Hint: show that using this rule we can give an incorrect semantics to a sequence of SIMP commands (compared with the intuitive meaning of sequential composition, or with the semantics obtained by using the abstract machine).

7. Using the big-step semantics of SIMP, prove by rule induction that if E is an integer expression in SIMP that uses only locations in m, then $\langle E, m \rangle \Downarrow n$ holds for a unique value n.

   Prove that also the values of boolean expressions working in a memory m are uniquely determined if the values of arithmetic expressions are.

8. Assume that in the definition of the big-step semantics of SIMP we replace the rule (seq) defining sequential composition by the following rule:

$$\frac{\langle C_1, s \rangle \Downarrow \langle skip, s' \rangle \quad \langle C_2, s \rangle \Downarrow \langle skip, s'' \rangle}{\langle C_1; C_2, s \rangle \Downarrow \langle skip, s'' \rangle}$$

where both C_1 and C_2 are evaluated in the state s. How is the semantics of the language affected by this change?

9. Assume that in the definition of the big-step semantics of SIMP without reference expressions, we replace the rule for the evaluation of

integer expressions:

$$\frac{\langle E_1, s \rangle \Downarrow \langle n_1, s' \rangle \quad \langle E_2, s' \rangle \Downarrow \langle n_2, s'' \rangle}{\langle E_1 \ op \ E_2, s \rangle \Downarrow \langle n, s'' \rangle} \ if \ n_1 \ op \ n_2 = n$$

by

$$\frac{\langle E_1, s \rangle \Downarrow \langle n_1, s \rangle \quad \langle E_2, s \rangle \Downarrow \langle n_2, s \rangle}{\langle E_1 \ op \ E_2, s \rangle \Downarrow \langle n, s \rangle} \ if \ n_1 \ op \ n_2 = n$$

Explain the consequences of this change in the semantics of SIMP.

10. Show, using the big-step semantics of SIMP, that the command

$$if \ False \ then \ C \ else \ C'$$

is equivalent to C' (i.e. both have the same semantics).

11. We add to the syntax of the language SIMP a post-test logically controlled loop:

$$\texttt{repeat C until B}$$

where the loop-body C will be repeated until the boolean expression B evaluates to True.

(a) Give a formal definition of the semantics of this command, by specifying the rules that should be added to the big-step semantics of SIMP.

(b) Show that this extension does not change the computational power of the language by giving a translation of

$$\texttt{repeat C until B}$$

in terms of the constructs that already exist in SIMP.

Part II

Functional Languages

Chapter 4

General Features of Functional Languages

The imperative programming languages we discussed in the previous part all share a common design idea: to make easier and more efficient use of von Neumann computers, basically by providing

- abstractions for the storage of data and programs, so that programmers do not need to keep track of memory addresses,

- input/output primitives that avoid complicated interactions with the operating system,

- control structures that make programs more readable and easier to write.

Although the level of abstraction provided by imperative languages varies greatly from assembly languages to sophisticated languages such as Java, there are common features in the design of all the imperative languages: they reflect the underlying machine architecture, and they emphasise the efficiency of the resulting code.

However, when developing software applications, efficiency is not always a priority. Depending on the application, properties such as low maintenance cost, easy debugging, or formally provable correctness, might have higher priority. For example, in safety-critical domains (such as medical, telecommunications, or transport systems) it is important to develop programs whose *correctness* can be certified (i.e. formally proved). Declarative languages, and in particular functional languages, can be a good alternative in this case.

Programs in functional languages are in general shorter, easier to understand, easier to design, debug and maintain than their imperative counterparts. For these reasons, functional programming languages are becoming increasingly popular in the industrial sector, although up to now only a minority of applications are written in declarative languages. The main domains of application of functional languages until now have been in artificial intelligence (for the implementation of expert systems), text processing (for instance, the UNIX editor emacs is implemented in LISP), graphical interfaces, natural language, telephony, music composition, symbolic mathematical systems, theorem provers and proof assistants.

LISP, which was introduced by J. McCarthy in the 50's, is considered to be the ancestor of functional programming languages. The syntax of LISP is based on lists (as the name of the language suggests: *LISt Processing*), and the atomic elements of lists are numbers and characters.

Although LISP is essentially an untyped language, and the first versions were dynamically scoped, its conciseness and elegance made it very popular. Since both data and programs are represented as lists, it is easy to define in LISP *higher-order functions*, that is, functions that take other functions as argument, or produce functions as result. This gives rise to a very different style of programming, and is one of the main features of functional languages. Several versions of LISP are in use, including Scheme [19], which is a small statically scoped language also untyped.

In recent years, several functional languages appeared which radically changed the syntax and introduced sophisticated type systems with type inference capabilities. Modern functional languages are *strongly typed* (which guarantees that no type errors will arise at run time), statically scoped, and have built-in memory management. ML and Haskell are examples of these, however they differ in their semantics: ML is *strict*, whereas Haskell is *lazy* which means that only computations that are needed to evaluate the program will be performed; we will discuss this point in more detail in the following sections. Another difference is that ML includes some imperative features (for efficiency reasons), whereas Haskell is a pure functional language enjoying *referential transparency*: the evaluation of an expression depends only on its components, and is therefore independent of its context.

The common feature of all functional languages is that programs consist of *functions* (as in the mathematical theory of functions, which is different from the notion of function used in imperative languages). As in mathematics, a function is a mapping between elements of two sets:

$$f : A \rightarrow B$$

indicates that the function f associates to each element of a given set A, called the *domain* of the function, an element of type B, called *codomain*. If a function f of type $A \rightarrow B$ is applied to an argument x of type A, it gives a result $(f\,x)$ of type B. With this approach, the focus is in *what* is to be computed, not *how* it should be computed. A function can be defined in terms of other functions previously defined by the programmer, taken from the libraries, or provided as language primitives.

For the examples in this part of the book we will use Haskell. It is freely available from the Internet: it can be downloaded, including the language report and user manual, from `www.haskell.org`. Hugs (the Haskell Users' Gofer System) is an interpreted version of Haskell. There are also compiled versions, for instance ghc (the Glasgow Haskell Compiler).

4.1 Defining Functions

The syntax of Haskell, ML, Clean, and most modern functional languages, is inspired by the definitions of functions in mathematics, using *equations* and *pattern-matching*. Patterns are expressions made out of variables and constructors. The latter can be predefined (such as the pair or list constructors) or can be defined by the programmer.

We will use a generic notation, similar to Haskell's syntax. We start by giving some examples.

Example 25 (Square) *We can compute the square of a number using a function* square *defined by the equation:*

```
square x = x * x
```

where we have used one of the predefined arithmetic functions (multiplication, written *)*. *The variable* x *in the left hand side of the equation is a pattern, indicating that we do not require arguments of any specific format. However, this does not mean that the function* square *can be applied to any kind of argument. If we do not include a type declaration, the type inference algorithm will be used and the system will infer that this is a function on numbers because we are using multiplication (more details are given in Section 4.4).*

Another traditional example is the function factorial, which can be defined in several ways.

Example 26 (Factorial) *First we use a conditional, where we test if the argument is 0 (the test for equality in Haskell is written* ==*).*

```
fact ::  Integer → Integer
fact n = if n == 0 then 1 else n * (fact (n - 1))
```

The program above consists of one equation, and we have included a type declaration specifying that we are defining a function from integers to integers. We can avoid the conditional and define factorial with two equations, using pattern-matching on the argument:

```
fact ::  Integer → Integer
fact 0 = 1
fact (n+1) = (n+1) * (fact n)
```

Or better, we can use conditional equations *(also called* guarded equations*), where we add guards to specify the conditions under which each equation can be applied; guards are evaluated in the order they appear:*

```
fact ::  Integer → Integer
fact n
    | n > 0    = n * (fact (n - 1))
    | n == 0   = 1
    | n < 0    = error "negative argument"
```

In the last example we used a predefined function, *error*, that takes a string as argument. When evaluated it causes immediate termination of the program and displays the string.

Another example of the use of guarded equations is in the definition of the function sign below.

Example 27 (Sign) *The function* sign *indicates whether its argument is positive, negative or zero.*

```
sign ::  Integer → Integer
sign x
    | x < 0    = -1
    | x == 0   = 0
    | x > 0    = 1
```

The definition of sign given above is equivalent to, but more readable than:

```
sign x = if x < 0 then -1 else if x == 0 then 0 else 1
```

One of the distinctive features of modern functional languages is that functions are also values even though we cannot display them or print them. We can therefore use functions as arguments or results for other (higher-order) functions. In Haskell all the functions are typed (although type declarations are optional), and the notation to associate a type to a function is:

$$f :: A \to B$$

where A and B are types. In particular, since a function can have another function as argument or result, the types A and B can be functional types of the form $A' \to B'$. Functional types are sometimes called *arrow types*.

The application of a function to an argument is denoted by juxtaposition, as in the examples above: `fact (n-1)` denotes the application of the function `fact` to the argument `(n-1)`. To avoid writing too many brackets in applications, there are some notational conventions:

- Application has precedence over other operations. For example, `square 3 + 1` means `(square 3) + 1`. To change the meaning of this expression we need brackets, as in `square (3 + 1)`.

- Application associates to the left. For example, `square square 3` is interpreted as `(square square) 3`.

  Note that this expression is ill-typed, since the function `square` expects an argument of type integer, not another function. We will show later how the type inference algorithm detects the error. We must use brackets in this case:

  `square (square 3)` is correctly typed.

- We will not write the outermost brackets. For example, we will write `square 3` instead of `(square 3)`

Another distinctive feature of functional programs is the use of recursion: in the definition of a function `f` we can use the function `f` itself. An example of recursive definition is the factorial function (see the definition of `fact` in Example 26). Recursion is the counterpart of iteration, which is one of the main control structures in imperative languages.

Before giving more details of the syntax of function definitions, we need to describe the mechanism by which programs are executed. The approach is radically different from that of imperative languages: for functional programming languages the role of the computer is to *evaluate and display the results* of the expressions that the programmer writes, using the functions defined in the program, in the libraries or the primitives of the language. As in mathematics, expressions may contain numbers, variables or names of functions. For instance 36, `square 6`, `6 * 6` are valid expressions. When we write an expression such as `square 6` the computer will display its result: 36. The process of evaluation is described in the next section.

4.2   Evaluation

To evaluate `square 6` the computer will use the definition of `square` in our program, that is, `square x = x * x`. Therefore the evaluator will replace the expression `square 6` by `6*6`. Then, using the predefined `*` operation, it will find the result 36.

The process of evaluating an expression is a *simplification process*, also called *reduction process* or *evaluation*. The goal is to obtain the *value* or irreducible form (also called *normal form*) associated to an expression, by a series of reduction steps. The *meaning* of an expression is its value.

We will denote a reduction step from the expression e to e' as follows:

$$e \rightarrow e'$$

Example 28 (Evaluating an Arithmetic Expression) *Consider   the expression*

$$(3 + 1) + (2 + 1).$$

We can simplify it as follows:

$$(3 + 1) + (2 + 1) \ \rightarrow \ (3 + 1) + 3 \ \rightarrow \ 4 + 3 \ \rightarrow \ 7.$$

Therefore 7 is the value denoted by the expression (3 + 1) + (2 + 1).

Note that there may be several reduction sequences for an expression. The following is also a correct reduction sequence for (3 + 1) + (2 + 1):

$$(3 + 1) + (2 + 1) \ \rightarrow \ 4 + (2 + 1) \ \rightarrow \ 4 + 3 \ \rightarrow \ 7$$

In this example we obtained in both cases the same value. This is a general property of functional programs.

Unicity of Normal Forms: *In (pure) functional languages the value of an expression is uniquely determined by its components, and is independent of the order of reduction.*

An obvious advantage of this property is improved readability of programs. It amounts to the referential transparency that was mentioned earlier.

Note also that not all the reduction sequences that start with a given expression lead to a value. This is not in contradiction with the previous property. It is caused by non-termination: some reduction sequences for a given expression may be infinite, but all the sequences that terminate reach the same value. This is more clearly seen with an example.

Example 29 (Non-Termination) *Let us define the constant function* fortytwo:

```
fortytwo x = 42
```

and the function infinity:

```
infinity = infinity + 1
```

It is clear that the evaluation of infinity *never reaches a normal form. The expression*

```
                    fortytwo infinity
```

gives rise to some reduction sequences that do not terminate, but those which terminate give the value 42 (unicity of normal forms).

The example above shows that although the normal form is unique, the order of reductions is important.

Definition 30 *A* strategy of evaluation *specifies the order in which reductions take place, in other words, it defines the reduction sequence that the language implements.*

The most popular strategies of evaluation for functional languages are:

1. *Call-by-Name (Normal order):* in the presence of a function application, first the definition of the function is used, then the arguments are evaluated if needed.

2. *Call-by-Value (Applicative order):* in the presence of a function application, first the arguments are evaluated, then the definition of the function is used to evaluate the application.

For example, using call-by-name, the expression fortytwo infinity is reduced in one step to the value 42, since this strategy specifies that the definition of the function `fortytwo` is used, which does not require the argument (it is a constant function). However, using call-by-value we must first evaluate the argument `infinity`, and as we already mentioned, the reduction sequence for this expression is infinite, hence we will never reach a normal form. Call-by-name guarantees that if an expression has a value, it will be reached.

As this example shows, different strategies of evaluation require different numbers of reduction steps, therefore the efficiency of a program (which is proportional to the number of reduction steps) depends on the strategy used. Some functional languages (for instance ML) use call-by-value, because if this strategy finds a value for a given expression, it does so in less steps than call-by-name (in general). This is because when an argument is used several times in the definition of a function, the call-by-value strategy will only evaluate it once.

Haskell uses a strategy called *lazy evaluation*, which is based on call-by-name. Since it is based on call-by-name, it guarantees that if an expression has a normal form, the evaluator will find it. In other words, it eliminates the risk of selecting a non-terminating reduction sequence when a finite one exists. However, to counter the potential lack of efficiency of a pure call-by-name strategy, Haskell uses sharing of subexpressions, that is, when an argument is used many times in a function definition, its evaluation is performed at most once, and the value is shared between all its occurrences.

Recursive definitions are evaluated by simplification, as any other expression. For instance, given the definition

```
fact :: Integer → Integer
fact n = if n == 0 then 1 else n * (fact (n - 1))
```

and the expression `fact 0`, the following is a possible evaluation sequence:

$$\begin{aligned}
\texttt{fact 0} \quad &\rightarrow \quad \text{if } 0 == 0 \text{ then } 1 \text{ else } 0 * (\texttt{fact } (0 - 1)) \\
&\rightarrow \quad \text{if True then } 1 \text{ else } 0 * (\texttt{fact } (0 - 1)) \\
&\rightarrow \quad 1
\end{aligned}$$

Note that the conditional (if-then-else) must be evaluated in a specific way to avoid non-termination:

1. First evaluate the condition.

2. If the result is True then evaluate *only* the expression in the left branch (`then`).

3. If the result is False then evaluate *only* the expression in the right branch (`else`).

Therefore the only reduction sequence for the expression `fact 0` is the one shown above, and this expression is terminating (there are no infinite reduction sequences).

However, this definition of `fact` does not treat correctly the case of negative arguments. For example, if we start reducing `fact (-1)` the sequence is infinite (the evaluation process does not terminate).

Using the version of factorial with conditional equations

```
fact ::  Integer → Integer
fact n
   | n > 0   = n * (fact (n - 1))
   | n == 0  = 1
   | n < 0   = error "negative argument"
```

this problem does not arise.

4.3   Building Functional Programs

Functions are the building blocks of functional languages. One way of combining functions is by *composition*, denoted by ·, as in the expression `f · g`. Composition is itself a function, which is predefined in functional languages. In Haskell it is defined as follows:

```
(·) ::  (β → γ) → (α → β) → (α → γ)
(f · g) x = f (g x)
```

The type of · indicates that we can only compose functions whose types are compatible. In other words, the composition operation · expects two functions f and g as arguments, such that the domain of f coincides with the codomain of g: the type of f is $(\beta \rightarrow \gamma)$ and the type of g is $(\alpha \rightarrow \beta)$, where α, β and γ are type variables representing arbitrary types.

The result of composing two functions f and g of compatible types $(\beta \rightarrow \gamma)$ and $(\alpha \rightarrow \beta)$ respectively, is a function of type $(\alpha \rightarrow \gamma)$: it accepts an argument x of type α (which will be supplied to g) and produces f (g x) which is in the codomain of f and therefore is of type γ.

Example 31 (Composition) *Consider the function* square *of Example 25. Since we have*

$$\text{square} :: \text{Integer} \rightarrow \text{Integer}$$

we can define a function quad *which computes the 4th power of a number as follows:*

```
quad = square · square
```

Arithmetic operations are also primitive functions, used in infix notation as in the expression 3 + 4. In Haskell we can use them in prefix notation if we enclose them in brackets, for example: (+) 3 4 .

The functions (+) and + have different types:

```
+ ::  (Integer, Integer) → Integer

(+) ::  Integer → Integer → Integer
```

The function (+) is the *Curryfied* version of +, that is, instead of working on *pairs* of numbers (i.e. two numbers provided simultaneously), it expects a number followed by another number. This might seem a small difference at first sight, but Curryfication (the word derives from the name of the mathematician Haskell Curry, after whom also the programming language is named) provides great flexibility to functional languages: for instance, we can use (+) to define functions such as successor.

```
successor ::  Integer → Integer
successor = (+) 1
```

Note that the expression + 1 is untypeable since + expects a pair of numbers as arguments. Therefore if we replace (+) by + in the previous definition of successor, the program is untypeable.

Another example in the same lines is the definition of the function double which doubles its argument:

```
double ::  Integer → Integer
double = (*) 2
```

Recall that there are some notational conventions to avoid writing too many brackets in arithmetic expressions:

- Application has priority over arithmetic operations. For example, square 1 + 4 * 2 should be read as (square 1) + (4 * 2).

- Subtraction associates to the left. For example, 3 - 1 - 2 is interpreted as (3 - 1)-2.

4.3.1 Local Definitions

As in mathematics, we can write:

```
f x = a * a where a = x/2
```

or equivalently,

```
f x = let a = x/2 in a * a
```

The words `let` and `where` are used to give structure to the program, introducing local definitions which are valid just on the right-hand side of the equation where they appear.

We can write several local definitions in one equation, as in the following example:

```
f x = square (successor x) where
        square z = z * z ; successor = (+) 1
```

If e is an expression that contains occurrences of a, which we denote as $e[a]$, the evaluation of expressions of the form:

$e[a]$ `where` $a = e'$

or

`let` $a = e'$ `in` $e[a]$

proceeds as follows:

1. evaluate the expression e', obtaining a result r;

2. replace the occurrences of a in e by r, obtaining an expression $e\{a \mapsto r\}$;

3. evaluate $e\{a \mapsto r\}$, that is, the expression e where every occurrence of a has been replaced by r, obtaining a result r'.

The value associated to the initial expression is r'.

Since the value of a is computed only once, the use of local definitions not only helps making programs more readable, but also more efficient.

4.4   Types: General Concepts

Types help in the design of software since they can be seen as a form of specification; in fact, there are powerful type systems in which types *are* complete specifications of programs, containing enough detail to allow the user to extract programs from them. However, at the moment these type systems are used mainly in sophisticated proof assistants; in most programming languages types are used as a *complement* to the program: they are concise descriptions of programs that serve primarily to detect errors at an early stage in the software development process. Types can also help the programmer in other ways, for instance they allow the compiler to perform code optimisations (some operations can be performed more efficiently if the types of the operands are known at compile time), and types can speed up the search for functions in the libraries (for example, if we know we need a function on integers, we will search only in the corresponding part of the library).

In a typed language, values are divided into classes according to the operations that can be performed on them, and each of these classes is called a type. Actually, in a typed functional language every valid expression (not only values) must have a type. Moreover, if an expression has a value (a normal form) the type of the expression should be the same as the type of its normal form.

Usually, typed programming languages come with a set of predefined types, which in most languages include basic types, such as numbers, booleans and characters. For example, in Haskell the set of predefined types includes:

- Basic data types: `Bool`, `Char`, `Int`, `Integer`, `Float`, `Double`, ... corresponding respectively to booleans, characters, small integers (single precision), big integers (arbitrary precision), single precision floating point numbers, and double precision floating point numbers (there are more numeric types in Haskell).

- Structured types: Tuples, Strings, Lists. Pairs are a particular case of tuples, the notation for tuples is: $(a_1, \ldots, a_n)$. Strings are sequences of characters, such as "Hello". A list type is denoted in Haskell as $[\alpha]$ where the α is replaced by the type of the elements of the list. For instance, `[Integer]` is the type of lists of integers.

- Function types: `Integer` $\rightarrow$ `Integer`, `Integer` $\rightarrow$ `Float`, $[\alpha]$ $\rightarrow$ `Integer`, (`Integer` $\rightarrow$ `Integer`)$\rightarrow$ `Integer`, are all examples of *arrow types*. By convention, arrows associate to the right, that is,

$$\text{Integer} \rightarrow \text{Integer} \rightarrow \text{Integer}$$

should be read as
$$\texttt{Integer} \to (\texttt{Integer} \to \texttt{Integer}).$$

Haskell is a static, strongly-typed language, that is, only expressions that will not generate type errors at run time are accepted for evaluation. Expressions that cannot be typed are considered erroneous and are rejected by the compiler or interpreter, prior to evaluation (of course a program that passes the type controls might not solve correctly the problem for which it has been built: the type system only guarantees that typeable programs are free of run time errors).

Since it is impossible to decide exactly which expressions are safe and which are not (i.e. the set of programs that may produce a type error at run time is not decidable), every static type checker will reject some programs that do not generate run time errors. Therefore a good type system for a statically typed programming language is one that offers a reasonable level of flexibility without compromising its correctness (i.e. without accepting programs that are unsafe). Modern functional languages have succeeded in this respect: they offer flexible type systems while filtering out all the programs with type errors before execution. This feature, together with the clarity and conciseness of the code, makes the software development process in functional languages shorter than in imperative languages in general.

One of the strengths of the type systems in modern functional languages is that they offer powerful type constructors, allowing the programmer to add to the language new types that suit the application that is being developed. This can be done by introducing *type definitions* in programs. Moreover, types may contain type variables that can be instantiated to (i.e. replaced by) arbitrary types, in other words, the type system is *polymorphic*. Another useful feature of modern functional languages is that they have a *type inference mechanism*, which frees the programmer from the need of writing type declarations for data and functions. We will discuss these points in the remaining sections.

4.5 Polymorphism

Type systems can be classified as *monomorphic* or *polymorphic* depending on the number of types that an expression can have. In a monomorphic language every expression has at most one type (the word monomorphic derives from the Greek meaning one form), whereas in a polymorphic language some expressions may have more than one type (polymorphic actually means many forms).

There are several ways of defining a polymorphic type system for a programming language:

1. we can use *generic types*, with type variables that can be instantiated to obtain several different types;

2. we can use *overloading*, where several different functions with different types share the same name;

3. we can use a *subtyping relation* and allow a program to be used with different subtypes of a given type.

The use of subtypes is typical of object-oriented languages. We will not discuss this technique in this book. In the rest of the section we will define and compare generic polymorphism and overloading.

Functional languages achieve polymorphism by using generic types, i.e. types with type variables. For example, the functional composition operator defined in Section 4.3 has type:

$$(\cdot) :: (\beta \to \gamma) \to (\alpha \to \beta) \to (\alpha \to \gamma)$$

where α, β, γ are type variables. This means that we can use the same composition operator in different situations, as the examples below show. One of the main advantages of this kind of polymorphism is that it allows the programmer to *reuse* code.

Example 32   *1. Consider again the function* quad *defined by:*

```
quad = square · square
```

Since square *is a function on integers as indicated by its type*

```
square ::  Integer → Integer
```

the operator · *is used in the definition of* quad *with type:*

```
(·)::(Integer → Integer) → (Integer → Integer) →
(Integer → Integer)
```

Therefore we can deduce that quad *is a function from integers to integers:*

```
quad ::  Integer → Integer.
```

But we can also define a function sqrt :: Integer → Float *to compute square roots of integers, and compose it with* square *using the* same *composition operator:*

$$\text{sqrt} \cdot \text{square}$$

This time the type of the composition operator is:

(·) ::(Integer → Float) → (Integer → Integer) → (Integer → Float)

2. *The* error *function used in the definition of factorial in Example 26:*

```
fact n
   | n > 0   = n * (fact (n - 1))
   | n == 0  = 1
   | n < 0   = error "negative argument"
```

is also polymorphic: error :: String → α. *In the definition of* fact *it is used with type* String → Integer.

Formally, the language of generic polymorphic types (we will call them just polymorphic types in the sequel) is defined as a set of *terms* built-out of *type variables* (α, β, γ, ...), and *type constructors* which are either atomic (for example: Integer, Float, ...) or take arguments. For example, the arrow is a type constructor that takes two arguments, as in String → α; the type constructor for lists requires just one argument, as in [α] (the polymorphic type of lists).

A polymorphic type represents the set of all its *instances*, obtained by substituting type variables by types. It is a very concise and elegant notation for a possibly infinite set of types. For example, [α] represents the set of all the types of lists, including [Integer] which corresponds to lists of integers, [[Integer]] which denotes lists of lists of integers, [Integer → Integer] which corresponds to lists of functions from integers to integers, etc.

Although generic polymorphism is typical of modern functional languages, imperative languages can also be designed to include this feature. For example, C++ uses type variables in *templates* to achieve polymorphism. The main difference between the approach of C++ and the approach of ML or Haskell is that C++ requires the programmer to write type declarations, whereas ML and Haskell can infer polymorphic types. We study type inference in the next section.

However, implementing generic polymorphism is not trivial, and it may cause some overheads at run time. For instance, the memory space required to store a polymorphic data structure depends on the actual type of the components; if this is not known at compile time, the compiler may solve the problem by introducing pointers (but this will make the access less efficient). Most imperative languages use only overloading, which is sometimes called *ad-hoc polymorphism*. Typical examples of overloaded operations are the arithmetic operations, that can be used both with integers or reals. The function that adds integers is different from the function that adds reals even if both are denoted by + (because the internal representation of these data differ: integers are represented as binary numbers, whereas reals are represented as exponent and mantissa). The compiler selects the function to be used according to the types of the operands, and generates code for the corresponding function (in contrast with generic polymorphism, where the *same* code is used with arguments of different types). Therefore, in the case of overloading, we do not achieve the goal of code reuse. Moreover, as programmers sometimes forget this difference ad-hoc polymorphism may lead to less clear programs. However, in the case of arithmetic operations we cannot write

$$+ \; :: \quad \alpha \to \alpha \to \alpha$$

since this would allow addition to be used with arguments of *any* type. Although there is no final solution to this problem, several alternatives have been proposed:

1. We could use different symbols for addition of integers and reals. For example, in the language Caml (a dialect of ML) we write + for addition of integers and +. for addition of reals.

2. We can enrich the language of types. For example, we could write type expressions such as
   + :: (Integer → Integer → Integer) ∧ (Float → Float → Float)
   with the intended meaning that + has both of these types.

3. We can define a notion of *type class*, as it is done in Haskell. For example, we can write:

$$(\text{+}) \; :: \quad \text{Num } \alpha \Rightarrow \alpha \to \alpha \to \alpha$$

which indicates that (+) has type $\alpha \to \alpha \to \alpha$ where α is in the class Num, that is, α is a type variable that can only be instantiated with numeric types.

4.6   Type Checking and Type Inference

Languages that are statically typed can use two kind of algorithms to detect type errors in programs: *type checking* or *type inference* algoritnms.

Most modern functional languages offer type inference mechanisms. In a language with type inference the programmer does not need to write types for the expressions used. If a type declaration is given, then it can be used to make type controls, but if there is no type declaration, then the type inference algorithm will try to "guess" (*infer*) a type for the program, based on the types of the primitive values and operations that appear in the program.

In contrast, a type checker requires that all types are declared. It reads the program and verifies that the types declared are compatible with the use of the different constructs in the language.

The first type inference algorithms were developed by R. Milner [9] for ML, based on the notion of types introduced by H. Curry for the λ-calculus. The λ-calculus provides a very elegant notation for function definition (λ-abstraction) and application, and serves as a theoretical model of computation for functional languages. The type system of ML not only introduced type inference, but also a form of generic polymorphism. Haskell's type system is based on similar ideas.

The type inference algorithm works roughly as follows. Given an expression to type:

- First the expression is decomposed into smaller subexpressions, and when a basic atomic expression is found (such as a constant, a variable, or a primitive operation), the information available is used (if it is a primitive of the language) or otherwise it is assigned the most general type possible (using type variables).

  For example, if the number 3.14 occurs in an expression, it will be assigned the type `Float`.

- Using the information gathered in the previous part, a set of type constraints is generated. Constraints are equations involving type variables. For example, if an expression contains the function `f` applied to the number 3.14, and `f` was given type α and 3.14 type `Float`, then we know that $\alpha = \texttt{Float} \to \beta$ for some type β, since the domain of the function must contain the number 3.14. The type of the application (`f 3.14`) should be β, the codomain of `f`.

  More precisely, the rules to generate types for functions and applications are the following:

(Function)

Given a function definition $f\ x_1 \ldots x_n$ = t, we assume that the formal arguments have arbitrary types $\sigma_1, \ldots, \sigma_n$ and try to obtain a type for the expression t. This is written:

$$x_1 :: \sigma_1, \ldots, x_n :: \sigma_n \vdash t :: \tau$$

which means that under the assumptions $x_1 :: \sigma_1, \ldots, x_n :: \sigma_n$, the expression t has type τ. From this we deduce a type for the function f:

$$\vdash f :: \sigma_1 \to \ldots \to \sigma_n \to \tau$$

Note that there are no assumptions for the type of f, since $\sigma_1, \ldots, \sigma_n$ are part of the arrow type (it is usual to omit the symbol $\vdash$ in this case).

(Application)

For any arbitrary set Γ of assumptions, if $\Gamma \vdash s :: \sigma \to \tau$ and $\Gamma \vdash t :: \sigma$ then

$$\Gamma \vdash (s\ t) :: \tau$$

This means that the domain of the function s should be the same as the type of t, and the result of the application should be in the codomain of the function.

In the same way, we can give rules describing how each kind of expression is typed. We need a rule for each predefined constant, function and operation, and also rules to type expressions including local definitions (we will study typing rules in Chapter 5).

• Finally, the type constraints are solved, using a unification algorithm (the details of this algorithm, which has also applications in logic programming languages, are given in Chapter 7). If no solution to the type constraints can be found, the expression is not typeable. Otherwise the most general solutions to the constraints are used in order to obtain the most general type associated to the given expression. Note that the type of the expression depends on the types of its components only.

A detailed description of the type inference algorithm and its implementation in Caml can be found in [2].

We now give some simple examples of type inference.

Example 33 *With the definition:*

```
square x = x * x
```

we can infer

```
square ::  Integer → Integer
```

assuming * *is an operation of type* (Integer,Integer) → Integer. *We proceed as follows: First the rule to type functions (see* (Function) *above) says that we need to obtain a type* τ *for* x * x *assuming* x ::σ *to deduce* square :: $\sigma \to \tau$. *The operation* * *requires arguments of type* Integer *(recall that the infix notation* x * x *is an abbreviation for* *(x,x)*). *Therefore, according to the rule* (Application), *we need* σ = Integer, *and* τ = Integer. *These constraints are trivially solvable, and we obtain*

```
square ::  Integer → Integer
```

If we now try to infer a type for the expression

```
square square 3
```

we obtain a set of unsolvable constraints: Since application associates to the left, the expression above is parsed as

```
(square square) 3
```

and since both occurrences of square *are associated with the type* Integer → Integer, *in order to obtain a type for the expression* (square square) *we need a solution for the equation* Integer = Integer → Integer. *Note that we are using the typing rule for application here, which says that the domain of the function must coincide with the type of the argument.*

The equation Integer = Integer → Integer *is obviously unsolvable. The type inference algorithm will then give an error message, indicating that the expression*

```
square square 3
```

cannot be typed since the function square *requires a number as argument, not a function.*

If a function is defined by several equations, we proceed as in the example above, generating a type from each equation. Since all the equations define the same function, a final constraint is added to indicate that all the types generated should coincide.

Example 34 *Consider the definition of factorial using guarded equations:*
```
fact n
    | n > 0   = n * (fact (n - 1))
    | n == 0  = 1
    | n < 0   = error "negative argument"
```

Since 0 is a primitive constant of type `Integer`, *from these equations we deduce that* n *is an integer, and moreover from the first and second equations we get:*

$$n \quad :: \quad \text{Integer}$$
$$\text{fact} \quad :: \quad \text{Integer} \rightarrow \text{Integer}$$

Similarly, since `error` *is a predefined function of type* `String` $\rightarrow \alpha$, *and* 0 *is a primitive constant of type* `Integer`, *from the third equation we obtain*

$$n \quad :: \quad \text{Integer}$$
$$\text{fact} \quad :: \quad \text{Integer} \rightarrow \alpha$$

Since the three equations define the same function, we must obtain a common type for `fact`. *In other words, we need to add a constraint:*

$$\text{Integer} \rightarrow \alpha = \text{Integer} \rightarrow \text{Integer}$$

The solution for this constraint is $\alpha = $ `Integer`, *therefore the type of* `fact` *is*

$$\text{Integer} \rightarrow \text{Integer}.$$

We give more examples of typing in Chapter 5 where we formally define the operational semantics and type system of a small language of recursive equations.

4.7 Type Definitions and Recursive Types (†)

In modern functional languages we can declare a new type by giving its name together with the operations that are used to build the values in the type. These operations are called *constructors* and can be monomorphic or polymorphic. There might be several constructors associated to a type, and moreover some of these constructors might use elements in the type to build new elements. In the latter case we say that the type is *recursive*.

We give first examples of non-recursive, monomorphic types.

Example 35 *We can define a type by enumerating its elements. A simple case is the type of booleans, with only two constructors:*

```
data Bool = True | False
```

In the same way, we can define a type of colours, with six constructors:

```
data Colours = Red | Blue | Yellow | Violet | Green | Orange
```

We can now define functions on colours using pattern-matching. For instance, the function that given a colour indicates its composition in terms of primary colours (red, blue and yellow) can be defined as follows:

```
decomposition ::  Colours -> [Colours]
decomposition Violet = [Red, Blue]
decomposition Green = [Blue, Yellow]
decomposition Orange = [Red, Yellow]
decomposition x = [x]
```

We can apply the function decomposition *to any colour. For example, the expression* decomposition Violet *gives the result* [Red,Blue] *and* decomposition Red *gives the result* [Red]. *The definition by pattern-matching above relies on the fact that patterns are considered in the order in which they appear in the program. If an argument for* decomposition *does not match any of the first three equations, then the fourth one will be used.*

A well-known example of a recursive type is the set of natural numbers.

Example 36 *We define the type* Nat *with two constructors:* Zero *and* Succ. *The latter takes an argument of type* Nat *(thus making the type recursive).*

```
data Nat = Zero | Succ Nat
```

The following expressions are values of type Nat:

```
Zero, Succ Zero, Succ (Succ Zero), ...
```

In this case the constructors are not polymorphic, but we can define in the same way types with polymorphic constructors, as in the following example.

Example 37 *The type of sequences can be defined as follows:*

```
Data Seq α = Empty | Cons α (Seq α)
```

The constructors are `Empty` *and* `Cons`*. The latter takes two arguments, the first one is of type* α*, and the second is a sequence of elements of the type* α*. This is a polymorphic type since* α *can be replaced by any type. For instance, we can define sequences of integers by instantiating* α *to* `Integer`*. The following expressions are values of type* `Seq Integer`*:*

- `Cons 3 Empty`, *which is a sequence containing just the element 3,*

- `Cons 3 (Cons 2 Empty)`, *which is a sequence containing the elements 3 and 2.*

We can define functions on sequences using pattern-matching. For instance, the function that indicates the number of elements in a sequence can be written:

```
length ::  (Seq α) → Integer
length Empty = 0
length (Cons x s) = 1 + (length s)
```

The type of sequences defined above is isomorphic to the type of lists, which is predefined in most modern functional languages. In Haskell, the empty list is denoted `[]`, and a non-empty list has the form `(x:l)` where x is the first element of the list (i.e. the *head*), and l is the list of the remaining elements (the *tail* of the list). It is usual to write values of the predefined type list using a shorthand notation: we can simply enumerate the elements of the list between square brackets, e.g. `[1,2,3,4]` instead of `1:(2:(3:(4:[])))`.

Example 38 (Transforming sequences into lists) *Any sequence can be transformed into a list (and vice-versa) simply by changing the constructors:*

```
toList ::  (Seq α) → [α]
toList Empty = []
toList (Cons x s) = (x:s)

toSeq ::  [α] → (Seq α)
toSeq [] = Empty
toSeq (x:l) = (Cons x l)
```

As the examples above show, constructors are used to build terms. What distinguishes a constructor from a function is that there is no definition associated to a constructor, and constructors can be used in patterns.

We end this section with an example of a higher-order function on sequences defined by pattern-matching.

Example 39 (Filter) *The function* filter *extracts from a given sequence all the elements that satisfy a certain predicate*[1]*:*

```
filter ::  (α → Bool) → (Seq α) → (Seq α)
filter p Empty = Empty
filter p (Cons x s) = if (p x) then (Cons x (filter p s))
                                else (filter p s)
```

Given a sequence of s *of numbers, we can obtain all its even numbers by evaluating the expression*

```
(filter even s)
        where even n = (n mod 2) == 0
```

If we want the even numbers that are smaller than 100, we can write

```
filter small (filter even s)
        where small n = n < 100
```

or better

```
filter smalleven s
        where smalleven n = (n < 100) and ((n mod 2) == 0)
```

Note that sequences can have an infinite number of elements. For instance, we can define the sequence of natural numbers:

```
nats = from 0
        where from n = Cons n (from (n+1))
```

Although we cannot expect to be able to build the sequence nats *in finite time, we can still use this sequence in a lazy language such as Haskell. For instance, to compute the sum of all the even natural numbers smaller than*

---

[1] filter is a predefined function on lists in most modern functional languages.

100, we can write:

```
sum (filter smalleven nats)
          where sum Empty = 0
                sum (Cons x s) = x + (sum s)
```

4.8   Reasoning about Programs (†)

All the values in a recursive data type are built using the constructors indicated in the data type definition. For this reason, to prove universal properties about programs involving recursive data types we can use the *Principle of Structural Induction* described in Chapter 1.

In the case of the type Nat defined above, the Structural Induction Principle coincides with the Principle of Mathematical Induction:

To prove a property P for all the values of type Nat we have to

1. Prove $P(Zero)$. This is the basis of the induction.

2. Prove that if $P(n)$ holds then $P(Succ\,n)$ holds. This is the *Induction Step*.

Example 40 (Proving Properties of Nat Programs) *The   following is a definition of addition on* Nat *by pattern-matching on the first argument:*

```
add Zero x = x
add (Succ x) y = Succ (add x y)
```

1. *We can prove by induction that* Zero *is a neutral element, that is, for every value* n *in* Nat*:*

$$\text{add Zero n = n = add n Zero}$$

The first equality, add Zero n = n, *is part of the definition of* add *(it is the first equation). To prove* n = add n Zero *we use induction.*

   (a) *Basis: We obtain* add Zero Zero = Zero *directly, using the definition of* add.

   (b) *Induction: By definition of* add:

$$\text{add (Succ n) Zero = Succ (add n Zero)}$$

   and the latter is equal to Succ n *as required, using the induction hypothesis.*

2. *We can also prove that* add *is commutative, that is, for every* n *and* m *in* Nat:

$$\text{add n m = add m n}$$

We proceed by induction on n:

(a) *Basis: Since we have just proved that* Zero *is a neutral element,*

$$\text{add Zero m = add m Zero = m.}$$

(b) *Induction: By definition of* add:

$$\text{add (Succ n) m = Succ (add n m)}$$

and by induction hypothesis,
$$\text{Succ (add n m) = Succ (add m n).}$$

Using the second equation in the definition of add *(from right to left!) we obtain* Succ (add m n) = add (Succ m) n. *To finish the proof we need a lemma:*

$$\text{add (Succ m) n = add m (Succ n)}$$

which we will also prove by induction (on m):

  i. *Basis: Note that*
    add (Succ Zero) n = Succ (add Zero n) = Succ n,
    and also add Zero (Succ n) = Succ n, *using the equations in the definition of* add.

  ii. *Induction: We have to prove that*
    add (Succ (Succ m)) n = add (Succ m) (Succ n).
    Using the second equation for add:
    add (Succ (Succ m)) n = Succ (add (Succ m) n)
    and we can now apply the induction hypothesis:
    Succ (add (Succ m) n) = Succ (add m (Succ n))
    and again use the second equation for add:
    Succ (add m (Succ n)) = add (Succ m) (Succ n),
    which completes the proof.

Example 41 (Proving Properties of Functions on Sequences) *To prove that the property:*

$$\text{length s < length (Cons x s)}$$

holds for all values s *of type* Seq α, *we use structural induction on the type*
Seq α.

1. *Basis: We have to prove the property for* Empty:

   length Empty = 0 *and*

   length (Cons x Empty) = 1 + length Empty = 1

2. *Induction: Assuming that* length s < length (Cons x s), *we have to prove*

$$\text{length (Cons y s)} < \text{length (Cons x (Cons y s))}$$

   for arbitrary y, x, s. *Using the definition of* length:

   length (Cons y s) = 1 + (length s)

   length (Cons x (Cons y s)) = 1 + (length (Cons y s)) = 2 + (length s)

   Therefore, assuming length s *is a number, the property holds. To complete the proof, again we can show by induction that the function* length *gives a result for any finite sequence, that is, for any value of type* Seq α *(the proof follows the same lines as above, and is omitted).*

We refer the reader to [1] for more examples.

4.9   Exercises

1. Define using a syntax similar to Haskell's:

   (a) a function min and a function max to compute the minimum and the maximum of two numbers, respectively.

   (b) a function fibonacci that takes a natural number n as input and gives the nth Fibonacci number as a result. Fibonacci numbers are generated by the recursive equation:

   $$Fib_n = Fib_{n-1} + Fib_{n-2}, \text{ with } Fib_0 = 0 \text{ and } Fib_1 = 1.$$

2. Write the definitions of quad (the function that computes the 4th power of a number), and double (the function that doubles its argument). Describe the reduction sequences for the expression:

$$\text{quad (double (3 + 1))}$$

using call-by-name (normal order) and call-by-value (applicative order).

3. What happens if we try to evaluate the expression:

```
sum (filter smalleven nats)
            where sum Empty = 0
                  sum (Cons x s) = x + (sum s)
```

given at the end of Example 39 in a language that uses a call-by-value strategy?

Write a functional program to add all the even numbers smaller than 100 assuming the call-by-value evaluation strategy will be used.

4. (a) Assume the function mult on natural numbers is defined by

```
mult x y = if x == 0 then 0 else x * y
```

where == is the equality test. Assume that e_1 == e_2 is evaluated by reducing e_1 and e_2 to normal form, and then comparing the normal forms.

Is mult commutative?

(b) Let infinity be the function defined by:

```
infinity = infinity + 1
```

What is the value of mult infinity 0?
And mult 0 infinity?

5. (a) Find a polymorphic type for the functions square, sign, fortytwo defined in this chapter.

(b) Find a polymorphic type for the functions quad, double defined previously.

6. (†) In Haskell we can define the type of polymorphic stacks as follows:

```
datatype Stack α = Empty | Push α (Stack α)
```

Write the usual functions `top` and `pop` on stacks (top gives the first element in the stack and pop eliminates the first element). Give a polymorphic type declaration for each function.

7. (†) A beginner Haskell programmer wrote the following program to add all the elements in a sequence of numbers:

```
sum Empty = 0
sum (Cons x s) = sum s
```

Even though there was no type error message, seeing the type that Haskell had displayed the programmer immediately realised that there was a bug in the program. Can you explain why?

Chapter 5

Operational Semantics of Functional Languages

In this chapter we will give a precise, formal description of the behaviour of programs in functional languages. For this we will use the same tool that we applied in the study of the operational semantics of imperative languages in Chapter 3: *transition systems*.

In order to isolate the important issues in the semantics of functional languages and avoid irrelevant details, we will define a small functional programming language working on integers and booleans, called SFUN.

Programs in SFUN are simply sets of recursive equations; each equation defines a function, using variables, numbers, booleans, operations on numbers and booleans (including a conditional), and other functions. A similar language based on recursive equations can be found in [21].

We will first define the (abstract) syntax of SFUN, and give a type system to filter out programs that are syntactically correct but contain type errors. We will use axioms and rules to specify the typing relation. Then we will give two alternative definitions of the operational semantics of SFUN, using the Structural Operational Semantics approach. More precisely, assuming programs are well-typed, we specify an evaluation relation between well-typed terms and values (integers and booleans) using first a call-by-value strategy, which we then modify to obtain a call-by-name language.

Finally, we will extend the language SFUN in two ways: we will include a let construct, which will allow us to write local definitions in terms and programs, and we will consider higher-order function definitions, that is, functions that take functional values as inputs or produce functions as output. We will show how the type system and the operational semantics can be extended to deal with this general class of programs.

5.1   Abstract Syntax of SFUN

To define the syntax of SFUN, we will assume that we have a set $\mathcal{V}$ of variables $\{x, y, z, x_1, x_2, \ldots\}$, and a set $\mathcal{F}$ of functions $\{f_1, \ldots, f_k\}$ with fixed arities. Functions will be defined by means of recursive equations in SFUN programs. The arity of a function corresponds to the number of arguments it takes. For instance, the function $\neg$ which will be used for negation on booleans is unary, whereas $\wedge$ (and) is binary. In general, we assume that the arity of f_i, denoted $ar(f_i)$, is $a_i \geq 0$.

The *terms* of the language SFUN are defined by the grammar:

$$
\begin{aligned}
t \quad &::= \quad n \mid b \mid x \mid t_1 \; op \; t_2 \mid t_1 \; bop \; t_2 \mid \neg t_1 \mid t_1 \wedge t_2 \mid \\
&\qquad \text{if } t_0 \text{ then } t_1 \text{ else } t_2 \mid f_i(t_1, \ldots, t_{a_i}) \\
op \quad &::= \quad + \mid - \mid * \mid / \\
bop \quad &::= \quad > \mid < \mid =
\end{aligned}
$$

where

- n represents integer numbers (constants),

- b represents booleans (*True*, *False*),

- x represents variables (in $\mathcal{V}$), and

- f_i denotes a function, to be defined in a program.

Note that for terms of the form $f_i(t_1, \ldots, t_{a_i})$, a_i could be 0, in which case we will omit the brackets and write just f_i.

We emphasise that the grammar above is defining the abstract syntax of the language, therefore the expressions in the grammar rules should be understood as labelled *trees*. The leaf nodes are labelled by numbers, booleans, and 0-ary function symbols. Non-leaf nodes are labelled by function symbols of arity greater than 0, by arithmetic or boolean operators, or by if-then-else (which can be seen as a primitive function symbol of arity 3).

Example 42 *The following are examples of terms in* SFUN.

- $2 * 3$ *is a term, and so is* $(2 * 3) + 4$. *Note that these are string representations of the corresponding syntax trees, we use brackets to avoid ambiguities.*

- *If* $ar(f_1) = 0$ *then* f_1 *is a term, and so is* $f_1 + 1$.

- $x > 0$ *is a term, and if* $ar(f_2) = ar(f_3) = 1$ *then*

$$\text{if } x > 0 \text{ then } f_2(x) \text{ else } f_3(x)$$

is a term.

We can now define programs in **SFUN**. Programs are used to define functions, by giving an equation for each function symbol $f_1, \ldots, f_k$. In the definition below, we will use the notation $Var(t)$ to represent the variables that occur in the term t. For instance, $Var(x) = \{x\}$, $Var(f_1(y, z)) = \{y, z\}$. If a term does not contain any occurrences of variables, we say that it is *closed*. For example, $f_2(True)$ is a closed term and so is $f_1 + 2$, but $x > 0$ is not closed.

Definition 43 (SFUN Program) *A program in* **SFUN** *is a set of recursive equations of the form:*

$$f_1(x_1, \ldots, x_{a_1}) = t_1$$
$$\vdots$$
$$f_k(x_1, \ldots, x_{a_k}) = t_k$$

such that

- $t_1, \ldots, t_k$ *are terms,*

- *for each* t_i $(1 \leq i \leq k)$, $Var(t_i) \subseteq \{x_1, \ldots, x_{a_i}\}$,

- *there is only one equation for each function* f_i *(where* $1 \leq i \leq k$*).*

Note that since equations are recursive, the terms t_i might contain occurrences of $f_1, \ldots, f_k$.

Example 44 *The following program* P *defines three functions, the first one has arity 0 and the others are unary.*

$f_1 = f_1 + 1$
$f_2(x) = 1$
$f_3(x) = x * x$

Comparing the syntax of function definitions in **SFUN** and the syntax *à la* Haskell that we used in the previous chapter, we notice that several simplifications have been made:

- patterns in **SFUN** are restricted to variables, therefore one equation is enough for each function;

- every function in SFUN works on tuples (with zero or more elements); there is no Curryfication;

- there are no local definitions in SFUN.

For example, the function *factorial* can be defined in SFUN with one equation, as follows:

$$\texttt{fact}(x) = \texttt{if } x = 0 \texttt{ then } 1 \texttt{ else } x * \texttt{fact}(x - 1)$$

5.2   A Type System for SFUN

The grammar defining the syntax of SFUN allows us to build terms such as $1 \wedge True$ which does not make sense. We will now define a type system which will be used to check (statically) terms and programs in SFUN, in order to filter out those containing type errors. Our goal is to obtain a *strongly typed* language, that is, a language in which every typeable term can be successfully evaluated (i.e. no errors can arise during the evaluation of well-typed terms).

The set of *types* for SFUN is defined by the following grammar:

$$
\begin{aligned}
b &\ ::=\ \ \textsf{int} \mid \textsf{bool} \\
\tau &\ ::=\ \ b \mid (b_1, \dots, b_n) \to b
\end{aligned}
$$

We have two basic types (int for integers and bool for booleans), and one type constructor (the arrow) which builds function types. A type of the form $(b_1, \dots, b_n) \to b$ is interpreted as the type of a function which takes n arguments of types $b_1, \dots, b_n$ and gives a result of type b. If $n = 1$ we will omit the brackets and simply write $b_1 \to b$.

The set of *well-typed terms* will be defined using a relation:

$$\Gamma \vdash_\varepsilon t : \tau$$

where

- Γ is called a *variable environment* or simply an environment, it associates variables with types. More precisely, Γ is a finite partial function from variables to types. We represent an environment Γ as a list $x_1 : \sigma_1, \dots, x_n : \sigma_n$ of pairs of variables and types, such that $\Gamma(x_i) = \sigma_i$.

- ε is a *function environment* assigning a type to each function, respecting its arity:

  If $arity(f_i) = a_i$ then $\varepsilon(f_i) = (\sigma_1, \dots, \sigma_i) \to \sigma$.

- t is a SFUN term.

- τ is a type.

The relation $\Gamma \vdash_\varepsilon t{:}\tau$ can be read as: *The term t has type τ under the assumptions in Γ and ε.* That is, assuming that each variable x in $dom(\Gamma)$ has type $\Gamma(x)$, and the functions $f_1, \ldots, f_k$ have types $\varepsilon(f_1), \ldots, \varepsilon(f_k)$, then the term t has type τ.

This relation is inductively defined by the system of axioms and rules shown in Figure 5.1. We have axioms specifying how to type numbers, booleans and variables (the environment is used to obtain types for variables). There is one rule for each arithmetic, comparison, and boolean operator, as well as rules indicating how to type conditionals and function applications. For the latter, the function environment is used to check that the types of the actual arguments are compatible with the type of the function.

We remark that all the types of functions are given in the environment ε: instead of infering the types of functions, we assume they have been declared by the programmer. For variables we do not require type declarations.

We will say that a term t is typeable if there is Γ and a type σ such that $\Gamma \vdash_\varepsilon t{:}\sigma$ can be derived using the axioms and rules given in Figure 5.1.

Example 45 *We give several examples of typeable terms below.*

1. *The term $x * x$ is typeable in any environment that associates the type int to the variable x. The following is a type derivation for this term, using the axioms and rules in Figure 5.1.*

$$
\cfrac{\cfrac{}{x{:}\text{int} \vdash_\varepsilon x{:}\text{int}}\ \text{(var)} \qquad \cfrac{}{x{:}\text{int} \vdash_\varepsilon x{:}\text{int}}\ \text{(var)}}{x{:}\text{int} \vdash_\varepsilon x * x{:}\text{int}}\ \text{(op)}
$$

2. *Assuming we have a function environment ε where $\varepsilon(f_1) = \text{int}$, the term $f_1 + 1$ is typeable (with type int). In particular, this term is typeable in an empty variable environment since it is closed (no assumptions for variables are needed). We can prove it as follows.*

$$
\cfrac{\cfrac{}{\vdash_\varepsilon f_1{:}\text{int}}\ \text{(fn)} \qquad \cfrac{}{\vdash_\varepsilon 1{:}\text{int}}\ \text{(n)}}{\vdash_\varepsilon f_1 + 1{:}\text{int}}\ \text{(op)}
$$

Axioms:

$$\frac{}{\Gamma \vdash_\varepsilon b\colon \mathsf{bool}}\ \text{(b)} \qquad \frac{}{\Gamma \vdash_\varepsilon n\colon \mathsf{int}}\ \text{(n)}$$

$$\frac{}{\Gamma \vdash_\varepsilon x\colon \sigma}\ \text{(var)} \quad \text{if } \sigma = \Gamma(x)$$

Rules:

$$\frac{\Gamma \vdash_\varepsilon t_1\colon \mathsf{int} \quad \Gamma \vdash_\varepsilon t_2\colon \mathsf{int}}{\Gamma \vdash_\varepsilon t_1\ op\ t_2\colon \mathsf{int}}\ \text{(op)}$$

$$\frac{\Gamma \vdash_\varepsilon t_1\colon \mathsf{int} \quad \Gamma \vdash_\varepsilon t_2\colon \mathsf{int}}{\Gamma \vdash_\varepsilon t_1\ bop\ t_2\colon \mathsf{bool}}\ \text{(bop)}$$

$$\frac{\Gamma \vdash_\varepsilon t_1\colon \mathsf{bool} \quad \Gamma \vdash_\varepsilon t_2\colon \mathsf{bool}}{\Gamma \vdash_\varepsilon t_1 \wedge t_2\colon \mathsf{bool}}\ \text{(and)} \qquad \frac{\Gamma \vdash_\varepsilon t\colon \mathsf{bool}}{\Gamma \vdash_\varepsilon \neg t\colon \mathsf{bool}}\ \text{(not)}$$

$$\frac{\Gamma \vdash_\varepsilon t_0\colon \mathsf{bool} \quad \Gamma \vdash_\varepsilon t_1\colon \sigma \quad \Gamma \vdash_\varepsilon t_2\colon \sigma}{\Gamma \vdash_\varepsilon \text{if } t_0 \text{ then } t_1 \text{ else } t_2\colon \sigma}\ \text{(if)}$$

$$\frac{\Gamma \vdash_\varepsilon t_1\colon \sigma_1 \quad \cdots \quad \Gamma \vdash_\varepsilon t_{a_i}\colon \sigma_{a_i}}{\Gamma \vdash_\varepsilon f_i(t_1, \ldots, t_{a_i})\colon \sigma}\ \text{(fn)} \quad \text{if } \varepsilon(f_i) = (\sigma_1, \ldots, \sigma_{a_i}) \to \sigma$$

Figure 5.1: Typing SFUN Terms

3. *The term* $x * \texttt{fact}(x - 1)$ *is typeable under the assumptions* x: int *and* $\varepsilon(\texttt{fact}) = $ int $\rightarrow$ int. *First we show that* $\texttt{fact}(x - 1)$ *is typeable:*

$$\cfrac{\cfrac{\cfrac{}{x\text{: int} \vdash_\varepsilon x\text{: int}} \text{(var)} \quad \cfrac{}{x\text{: int} \vdash_\varepsilon 1\text{: int}} \text{(n)}}{\cfrac{x\text{: int} \vdash_\varepsilon x - 1\text{: int}}{} \text{(op)}}}{x\text{: int} \vdash_\varepsilon \texttt{fact}(x - 1)\text{: int}} \text{(fn)}$$

Since x *is trivially typeable under the assumption* x: int, *using the rule* (op) *we obtain:*

$$x\text{: int} \vdash_\varepsilon x * \texttt{fact}(x - 1)\text{: int}$$

4. *The term*

$$\texttt{if } x = 0 \texttt{ then } 1 \texttt{ else } x * \texttt{fact}(x - 1)$$

is typeable if $\varepsilon(\texttt{fact}) = $ int $\rightarrow$ int *and* $\Gamma(x) = $ int. *First we show that* $x = 0$ *is typeable in the environment* x: int.

$$\cfrac{\cfrac{}{x\text{: int} \vdash_\varepsilon x\text{: int}} \text{(var)} \quad \cfrac{}{x\text{: int} \vdash_\varepsilon 0\text{: int}} \text{(n)}}{x\text{: int} \vdash_\varepsilon x = 0\text{: bool}} \text{(bop)}$$

We have also shown (above) that $x * \texttt{fact}(x - 1)$ *is typeable in the same environment, and using the axiom* (n) *we can derive:*

$$x\text{: int} \vdash_\varepsilon 1\text{: int}$$

Therefore, we can use the rule (if) *to obtain a type derivation for our initial term:*

$$\cfrac{x\text{: int} \vdash_\varepsilon x = 0\text{: bool} \quad x\text{: int} \vdash_\varepsilon 1\text{: int} \quad x\text{: int} \vdash_\varepsilon x * \texttt{fact}(x-1)\text{: int}}{x\text{: int} \vdash_\varepsilon \texttt{if } x = 0 \texttt{ then } 1 \texttt{ else } x * \texttt{fact}(x - 1)\text{: int}} \text{(if)}$$

Programs in SFUN will be type-checked to ensure that each function definition is compatible with the type declared for the function in the environment ε: both sides of each equation should have the same type.

Definition 46 (Typing SFUN Programs) *A program* P *in* SFUN:

$$f_1(x_1, \ldots, x_{a_1}) \quad = \quad t_1$$
$$\vdots$$
$$f_k(x_1, \ldots, x_{a_k}) \quad = \quad t_k$$

is typeable if for each equation $f_i(x_1, \ldots, x_{a_i}) = t_i$ *there is a type* τ_i *and an environment* Γ_i *such that*

$$\Gamma_i \vdash_\varepsilon f_i(x_1, \ldots, x_{a_i})\text{: } \tau_i \quad and \quad \Gamma_i \vdash_\varepsilon t_i\text{: } \tau_i.$$

Example 47 *We give examples of typeable programs below.*

1. *The program P of Example 44:*

$$f_1 = f_1 + 1$$
$$f_2(x) = 1$$
$$f_3(x) = x * x$$

is typeable in an environment ε where

$$\varepsilon(f_1) = \mathsf{int}$$
$$\varepsilon(f_2) = \mathsf{int} \to \mathsf{int}$$
$$\varepsilon(f_3) = \mathsf{int} \to \mathsf{int}$$

To prove that P is correctly typed, we must type-check each equation. The left-hand side of the first equation is the term f_1 of type int; in our system this is written

$$\vdash_\varepsilon f_1 \colon \mathsf{int}.$$

The right-hand side is the term $f_1 + 1$, which also has type int (see Example 45, where we proved $\vdash_\varepsilon f_1 + 1 \colon \mathsf{int}$). Therefore the first equation is well typed.

Similarly, we can show that the second equation type-checks: using the axiom (var) *and the rule* (fn) *we obtain $x \colon \mathsf{int} \vdash_\varepsilon f_2(x) \colon \mathsf{int}$, and using the axiom* (n) *we obtain $x \colon \mathsf{int} \vdash_\varepsilon 1 \colon \mathsf{int}$.*

To see that the third equation is correctly typed, recall that

$x \colon \mathsf{int} \vdash_\varepsilon x * x \colon \mathsf{int}$ (see Example 45),

and given $\varepsilon(f_3) = \mathsf{int} \to \mathsf{int}$ we can easily deduce $x \colon \mathsf{int} \vdash_\varepsilon f_3(x) \colon \mathsf{int}$.

2. *The program*

$$\mathtt{fact}(x) = \mathtt{if}\ x = 0\ \mathtt{then}\ 1\ \mathtt{else}\ x * \mathtt{fact}(x-1)$$

is typeable if $\varepsilon(\mathtt{fact}) = \mathsf{int} \to \mathsf{int}$: we have already proved (see Example 45) that

$$x \colon \mathsf{int} \vdash_\varepsilon \mathtt{if}\ x = 0\ \mathtt{then}\ 1\ \mathtt{else}\ x * \mathtt{fact}(x-1) \colon \mathsf{int}$$

and we obtain $x \colon \mathsf{int} \vdash_\varepsilon \mathtt{fact}(x) \colon \mathsf{int}$ easily using rule (fn) *and axiom* (var).

The type system of SFUN is syntax directed: the form of the term indicates the rules that need to be applied in order to type-check it. It also has the property of *unicity of types*: there is at most one type for a given term t in a given Γ and ε. Formally:

Unicity of Types: *For any* SFUN *term* t, *if* $\Gamma \vdash_\varepsilon t : \sigma$ *and* $\Gamma \vdash_\varepsilon t : \tau$ *then* $\sigma = \tau$.

We can prove this property by rule induction (see the exercises at the end of the chapter).

Since types do not contain type variables, this property indicates that the system is monomorphic. In order to define a polymorphic type system, we can include type variables in the definition of types and generalise the typing rules so that functions could be applied to arguments with types that are instances of the types declared in the environment. We will not develop the system further in this direction, instead, in Section 5.4 we will extend it in order to type additional language constructs.

5.3 Operational Semantics of SFUN

In this section we assume that programs and terms are well-typed. We will give two alternative definitions for the semantics of SFUN: first we will model a *call-by-value* evaluation strategy (also called *applicative order* of reduction), then we will modify the transition system to follow a *call-by-name* strategy (*normal order* of reduction).

First, note that open terms do not have a meaning in themselves, since they contain variables whose values are not defined. Also, it is clear that we cannot give a meaning to SFUN terms in isolation. We need to take into account the program, which gives meanings to the function symbols that appear in terms. We will therefore define the semantics of *closed* terms in the context of a given program P:

$$f_1(x_1, \ldots, x_{a_1}) = d_1$$
$$\vdots$$
$$f_k(x_1, \ldots, x_{a_k}) = d_k$$

We will specify two *evaluation relations* for closed terms in SFUN. In other words, we will define two alternative big-step semantics for the language SFUN. In both cases *configurations* will simply be terms, and values will be constants (numbers and booleans). The evaluation relations will be denoted by $\Downarrow_P^V$ and $\Downarrow_P^N$ to emphasise the fact that the value of a term depends on the given program P and the strategy that we follow.

5.3.1   Call-by-Value Semantics of SFUN

In Figure 5.2 we give an inductive definition, using a set of axioms and rules, of the evaluation relation $\Downarrow_P^V$. The expression $t \Downarrow_P^V v$ indicates that the term t evaluates to v under call-by-value using the program P.

SFUN constants (integers and booleans) are already values, as the axioms (n) and (b) indicate. The rules for arithmetic and boolean operators are standard. We have two rules for the if-then-else, since depending on the value of the condition we need to evaluate either the then branch or the else branch. The rule (fn) indicates how function applications are evaluated, and it is here that we see that a call-by-value strategy is in place: the arguments of the function are evaluated first, and then the definition of the function is used (d_i is the right-hand side of the corresponding equation) replacing the formal arguments with the values of the actual arguments. We use the notation $d_i\{x_1 \mapsto v_1, \ldots, x_{a_i} \mapsto v_{a_i}\}$ to represent the term obtained after replacing (simultaneously) in d_i each occurrence of x_1 by v_1, x_2 by v_2, etc.

Again, we observe that the system is syntax-directed: given a term to evaluate (i.e. a labelled syntax tree), the labels in the tree indicate the rules or axioms that should be applied.

We now give some examples of evaluation.

Example 48 *First we evaluate terms with respect to the program P consisting of the three equations:*

$$f_1 = f_1 + 1$$
$$f_2(x) = 1$$
$$f_3(x) = x * x$$

1. *The term $f_2(0)$ has the value 1, more precisely: $f_2(0) \Downarrow_P^V 1$. This can be shown as follows, using the axioms and rules in Figure 5.2:*

$$\frac{\dfrac{}{0 \Downarrow_P^V 0}\ (n) \qquad \dfrac{}{1\{x \mapsto 0\} \Downarrow_P^V 1}\ (n)}{f_2(0) \Downarrow_P^V 1}\ (fn)$$

2. *With the same program, the term $f_2(f_1)$ does not have a value: there is no v such that $f_2(f_1) \Downarrow_P^V v$. This is because to evaluate $f_2(f_1)$ we must use rule (fn), which requires the evaluation of f_1 first. But to find a value for f_1 we must use again rule (fn), which requires a value for $f_1 + 1$.*

$$\frac{}{n \Downarrow_P^V n} \; \text{(n)} \qquad \frac{}{b \Downarrow_P^V b} \; \text{(b)}$$

$$\frac{t_1 \Downarrow_P^V n_1 \quad t_2 \Downarrow_P^V n_2}{t_1 \; op \; t_2 \Downarrow_P^V n \quad \text{if } n = n_1 \; op \; n_2} \; \text{(op)}$$

$$\frac{t_1 \Downarrow_P^V n_1 \quad t_2 \Downarrow_P^V n_2}{t_1 \; bop \; t_2 \Downarrow_P^V b \quad \text{if } b = n_1 \; bop \; n_2} \; \text{(bop)}$$

$$\frac{t_1 \Downarrow_P^V b_1 \quad t_2 \Downarrow_P^V b_2}{t_1 \wedge t_2 \Downarrow_P^V b \quad \text{if } b = b_1 \; and \; b_2} \; \text{(and)} \qquad \frac{t \Downarrow_P^V b}{\neg t \Downarrow_P^V b' \quad \text{if } b' = not \; b} \; \text{(not)}$$

$$\frac{t_0 \Downarrow_P^V True \quad t_1 \Downarrow_P^V v_1}{\text{if } t_0 \text{ then } t_1 \text{ else } t_2 \Downarrow_P^V v_1} \; \text{(If}_\text{T})$$

$$\frac{t_0 \Downarrow_P^V False \quad t_2 \Downarrow_P^V v_2}{\text{if } t_0 \text{ then } t_1 \text{ else } t_2 \Downarrow_P^V v_2} \; \text{(If}_\text{F})$$

$$\frac{t_1 \Downarrow_P^V v_1 \quad \ldots \quad t_{a_i} \Downarrow_P^V v_{a_i} \quad d_i\{x_1 \mapsto v_1, \ldots, x_{a_i} \mapsto v_{a_i}\} \Downarrow_P^V v}{f_i(t_1, \ldots, t_{a_i}) \Downarrow_P^V v} \; \text{(fn)}$$

Figure 5.2: Call-by-Value Evaluation

3. *With the same program, $f_3(2+1)$ has the value 9. This is shown as follows:*

$$\cfrac{\cfrac{}{2 \Downarrow_P^V 2}\,(n) \quad \cfrac{}{1 \Downarrow_P^V 1}\,(n)}{\cfrac{2+1 \Downarrow_P^V 3}{}}\,(op) \qquad \cfrac{\cfrac{\cfrac{}{3 \Downarrow_P^V 3}\,(n) \quad \cfrac{}{3 \Downarrow_P^V 3}\,(n)}{x * x\{x \mapsto 3\} \Downarrow_P^V 9}\,(op)}{f_3(2+1) \Downarrow_P^V 9}\,(fn)$$

Example 49 *In the previous chapter we gave an informal description of call-by-value and call-by-name evaluation, and we showed an evaluation sequence for* (fact 0), *giving the value 1. Using the* SFUN *program P defining the function factorial:*

$$\texttt{fact}(x) = \text{if } x = 0 \text{ then } 1 \text{ else } x * \texttt{fact}(x - 1)$$

we can prove that fact(0) *evaluates to 1 under call-by-value:*

$$\cfrac{\cfrac{}{0 \Downarrow_P^V 0}\,(n) \quad \cfrac{\cfrac{\cfrac{}{0 \Downarrow_P^V 0}\,(n) \quad \cfrac{}{0 \Downarrow_P^V 0}\,(n)}{0 = 0 \Downarrow_P^V True}\,(bop) \quad \cfrac{}{1 \Downarrow_P^V 1}\,(n)}{\text{if } 0 = 0 \text{ then } 1 \text{ else } 0 * \texttt{fact}(0 - 1) \Downarrow_P^V 1}\,(If_T)}{\texttt{fact}(0) \Downarrow_P^V 1}\,(fn)$$

5.3.2 Properties of SFUN

First of all we remark that the operational semantics of SFUN and the type system are consistent: the evaluation relation preserves types.

Type Preservation: *If t is a* SFUN *term of type σ, and $t \Downarrow_P^V v$, then v is a value of type σ.*

This property (also called Subject Reduction) can be proved by rule induction. The proof is left as an exercise.

Another important property of SFUN is that there is *at most one* value associated to a closed term in the context of a given program. In other words, the semantics of SFUN is *deterministic*. Moreover, if a closed term is typeable then the evaluation process cannot produce type errors: SFUN is a *strongly typed language*. However, since recursive functions may be undefined for certain arguments, we cannot guarantee that any closed typeable term has a value. If the program under consideration is non-recursive, then typeability does guarantee the existence of values. Combined, these properties imply that any closed typeable term in a non-recursive typeable SFUN program has one and only one value.

Strong Typing and Determinism: *The evaluation of a closed, typeable term t, in the context of a typeable program P, cannot produce type errors. Moreover, if $t \Downarrow_P^V v_1$ and $t \Downarrow_P^V v_2$ then $v_1 = v_2$.*

This property can be proved by rule induction.
Basis:

- If t is a number n then $n \Downarrow_P^V n$ using the axiom (n), and this is the only axiom or rule that applies.

- If t is a boolean b then $b \Downarrow_P^V b$ using the axiom (b), and this is the only axiom or rule that applies.

In both cases the evaluation is successful and there is only one possible result.

There are no other base cases to consider because t is closed (it cannot be a variable).
Induction:

We distinguish cases according to the rule applied (which is determined by t).

- If there is an operator at the root of t, then we will apply one of the rules (op), (bop), (and), (not), depending on the operator (only one rule applies). We will only show the case where t is a term of the form $t_1 + t_2$ (the other cases are similar). In this case t_1, t_2 and t are terms of type int. By induction, the evaluation of t_1 and t_2 cannot produce type errors, and there is at most one value v_1 such that $t_1 \Downarrow_P^V v_1$, and one value v_2 such that $t_2 \Downarrow_P^V v_2$. Since evaluation preserves types, v_1 and v_2 are integer values. Hence $v_1 + v_2$ is defined, and $t \Downarrow_P^V v$ where $v = v_1 + v_2$, using the rule for $+$.

- In the case of a conditional if t_1 then t_2 else t_3, since the term is typeable we know that t_1 is a term of boolean type and t_2, t_3 have both a certain type σ. By induction the evaluation of the terms t_1, t_2, and t_3 does not produce errors, and t_1, t_2, t_3 have at most one value each: v_1, v_2 and v_3. Since the evaluation relation preserves types, v_1 is a boolean constant. If v_1 is *True*, we can only apply the rule (If$_T$), and the value of t is v_2. Otherwise, we apply the rule (If$_F$) and the value of t is v_3. In both cases the value is uniquely determined.

- Finally, if t is a function application $f_i(t_1, \ldots, t_{a_i})$, then using the rule (fn):

$f_i(t_1, \ldots, t_{a_i}) \Downarrow_P^V v$ if and only if

$t_1 \Downarrow_P^V v_1, \ldots, t_{a_i} \Downarrow_P^V v_{a_i}, d_i\{x_1 \mapsto v_1, \ldots, x_{a_i} \mapsto v_{a_i}\} \Downarrow_P^V v.$

By induction hypothesis, there is at most one value for the terms $t_1, \ldots, t_n$ and for $d_i\{x_1 \mapsto v_1, \ldots, x_{a_i} \mapsto v_{a_i}\}$, and the evaluation of these terms does not produce errors. Therefore the value of t is uniquely determined. This completes the proof.

5.3.3   Call-by-Name Semantics of SFUN

The evaluation relation defined in the previous section proceeds in a call-by-value fashion. In order to model a call-by-name strategy we have to change the rule (fn) that defines the behaviour of application. We will specify a binary relation between closed terms and values in the context of a SFUN program P, denoted $t \Downarrow_P^N v$, meaning that the term t evaluates to v under call-by-name using the program P. We use the super-index N to distinguish this evaluation relation from the one studied in the previous sections.

To define the relation $\Downarrow_P^N$ we use the rules and axioms of Figure 5.2 (replacing $\Downarrow_P^V$ by $\Downarrow_P^N$), except for rule (fn) which is replaced by the following rule:

$$\frac{d_i\{x_1 \mapsto t_1, \ldots, x_{a_i} \mapsto t_{a_i}\} \Downarrow_P^N v}{f_i(t_1, \ldots, t_{a_i}) \Downarrow_P^N v} \text{ (fn}_\text{N})$$

where d_i is the right-hand side of the equation defining f_i in the program P.

This rule indicates that the result of the application of the function f_i to the arguments $t_1, \ldots, t_{a_i}$ is obtained by using the equation defining f_i in P where the formal parameters $x_1, \ldots, x_{a_i}$ are replaced by the actual arguments $t_1, \ldots, t_{a_i}$. In contrast, the call-by-value evaluation relation uses the values of the actual arguments.

The system is still deterministic, and strongly typed:

Strong Typing and Determinism: *The call-by-name evaluation of a closed, typeable term t, in the context of a typeable program P, does not produce type errors. Moreover, if $t \Downarrow_P^N v_1$ and $t \Downarrow_P^N v_2$ then $v_1 = v_2$.*

The proof is similar to the one given in the previous section for $\Downarrow_P^V$.
We now give some examples of call-by-name evaluation.

Example 50 *Consider again the program P:*

$$f_1 = f_1 + 1$$
$$f_2(x) = 1$$
$$f_3(x) = x * x$$

1. *With this program, the term $f_2(0)$ has the value 1, that is, $f_2(0) \Downarrow_P^N 1$. To see this we use the definition of the evaluation relation:*

$$\frac{\dfrac{}{1\{x \mapsto 0\} \Downarrow_P^N 1} \text{(n)}}{f_2(0) \Downarrow_P^N 1} \text{(fn}_\text{N})$$

2. *With the same program, $f_2(f_1)$ also has the value 1. This is in contrast with the call-by-value semantics (see Example 48) in which this term does not have a value. We prove that $f_2(f_1) \Downarrow_P^N 1$ as follows:*

$$\frac{\dfrac{}{1\{x \mapsto f_1\} \Downarrow_P^N 1} \text{(n)}}{f_2(f_1) \Downarrow_P^N 1} \text{(fn}_\text{N})$$

Note that the function f_2 does not use its argument. In this case, $1\{x \mapsto f_1\} = 1$ and hence the actual argument f_1 is not evaluated (avoiding in this way an infinite computation). This is a general property of the call-by-name semantics: if a term has a value, the call-by-name strategy will find it.

3. *With the same program, the term $f_3(2 + 1)$ has the value 9 (compare with the call-by-value semantics in Example 48). We show it as follows:*

$$\frac{\dfrac{\dfrac{}{2 \Downarrow_P^N 2} \text{(n)} \quad \dfrac{}{1 \Downarrow_P^N 1} \text{(n)}}{2 + 1 \Downarrow_P^N 3} \text{(op)} \quad \dfrac{\dfrac{}{2 \Downarrow_P^N 2} \text{(n)} \quad \dfrac{}{1 \Downarrow_P^N 1} \text{(n)}}{2 + 1 \Downarrow_P^N 3} \text{(op)}}{\dfrac{x * x\{x \mapsto 2 + 1\} \Downarrow_P^N 9}{f_3(2 + 1) \Downarrow_P^N 9} \text{(fn}_\text{N})} \text{(op)}$$

Here, according to rule (fn$_\text{N}$) we have to evaluate $x * x\{x \mapsto 2 + 1\}$, which represents the term $(2 + 1) * (2 + 1)$. We see that the argument

(2+1) is copied and then evaluated twice. The call-by-value semantics is more efficient in this case, because instead of copying the argument, it copies the value 3. This is a general property of the call-by-value strategy: arguments are evaluated only once, even if they are used several times.

Under the call-by-name semantics, if an argument is used more than once in a function its evaluation is repeated. To avoid this source of inefficiency, languages that implement a call-by-name strategy (e.g. Haskell) use *sharing*. Call-by-name with sharing is known as *lazy evaluation*. The idea is to represent terms in the right-hand side of equations as graphs, where repeated occurrences of variables are represented via pointers to a unique variable node. In this way, actual arguments are not copied: a substitution operation replaces the unique variable node by the actual argument, and when it is evaluated (if it is needed), the value obtained is shared.

5.4   Extensions of SFUN

In the previous sections we assumed that programs consist of equations defining a set of *global* functions, which are all available to be used in terms. We will now define an extension of the language SFUN in which it will be possible to introduce *local* definitions, using the keyword `let`. Moreover, functions will be allowed to take other functions as input, or to produce functions as a result. Functions will become first class values.

Recall the standard syntax for local definitions in functional languages (see Chapter 4):

```
let x = expression1 in expression2
```

Using a `let` construct, we can write terms containing local identifiers, for example:

```
let y = x*x in y*y
```

and use them in equations, such as

```
f x = let y = x*x in y*y
```

We will also add a `let fun` construct to define local functions. For instance, we can write

```
let fun square x = x*x in (square 3)
```

Actually, the same `let` construct could be used to define local identifiers or local functions, however, to make programs easier to understand we prefer to use two different keywords. We will assume that definitions using `let` are *not* recursive, whereas a function defined via a `let fun` may be recursive.

We will extend the abstract syntax of SFUN to take into account these changes. The extended language will be called FUN. We will also adapt the type system and operational semantics to deal with the new language constructs.

5.4.1   Abstract Syntax of FUN

The following grammar defines the syntax of terms in FUN.

$$
\begin{aligned}
t \quad ::= \quad & n \mid b \mid x \mid f \mid op \mid bop \mid \neg \mid \wedge \mid \\
& \text{if } t_0 \text{ then } t_1 \text{ else } t_2 \mid (t_1\ t_2) \mid \\
& \text{let } x = t_1 \text{ in } t_2 \mid \text{let fun } f\ x_1 \ldots x_n = t_1 \text{ in } t_2 \\
op \quad ::= \quad & + \mid - \mid * \mid / \\
bop \quad ::= \quad & > \mid < \mid =
\end{aligned}
$$

In addition to the integer and boolean constants (denoted n, b in the grammar, as before) and variables (denoted by x) we also have functions (denoted by f) and operators as basic terms. This reflects the fact that functions are now values on their own. A term of the form $(t_1\ t_2)$ represents the application of t_1 to t_2 (we could write $Ap(t_1, t_2)$ but to simplify the notation the application operator is omitted). The let expressions are as discussed above. Note that functions and operators are Curryfied (see Chapter 4).

As usual we omit brackets whenever possible, writing $s\ t_1 \ldots t_n$ instead of $(\ldots (s\ t_1)\ t_2) \ldots t_n)$; application associates to the left. To make FUN programs more readable, we will write binary operators in infix notation as in SFUN, i.e. we write $(t_1\ op\ t_2)$ instead of $op\ t_1\ t_2$.

Programs in FUN are sets of recursive equations defining global functions, which are Curryfied:

$$
\begin{aligned}
f_1\ x_1 \ldots x_{a_1} \quad &= \quad t_1 \\
&\vdots \\
f_k\ x_1 \ldots x_{a_k} \quad &= \quad t_k
\end{aligned}
$$

where

- $t_1, \ldots, t_k$ are FUN terms,

- for each t_i $(1 \leq i \leq k)$, $Var(t_i) \subseteq \{x_1, \ldots, x_{a_i}\}$,

- there is only one equation for each global function f_i $(1 \leq i \leq k)$.

The terms t_i might contain occurrences of $f_1, \ldots, f_k$ since the equations are recursive.

5.4.2   A Type System for FUN

To type terms and programs containing local definitions we need to generalise the type system of SFUN. The set of types has to include general arrow types, in order to take into account the existence of higher-order functions. Types are defined by the following grammar:

$$\tau ::= \mathsf{int} \mid \mathsf{bool} \mid \tau \to \tau$$

As usual, we use brackets in the textual notation to avoid ambiguities, for instance we write (int $\to$ int) $\to$ int for the type of functions that take a function from integers to integers as input and produce an integer as a result. To avoid writing too many brackets, we assume arrows associate to the right (as indicated in Chapter 4).

We will assume that local function definitions in FUN are explicitly typed (type inference in this general setting is out of the scope of this book). For this, we add type declarations in `let fun` constructs, using the syntax:

$$\mathtt{let\ fun}\ f\ x_1 : \sigma_1 \ldots x_n : \sigma_n = t_1 : \sigma\ \mathtt{in}\ t_2$$

We need to provide the type σ for t_1 because f could appear in t_1 (in a recursive definition).

We will define a typing relation $\Gamma \vdash t : \tau$ where

- Γ is an environment associating identifiers (variables and functions) with types,

- t is a FUN term, and

- τ is a type as defined by the grammar above.

Note that, in contrast with the type system for SFUN, the environment Γ now contains type assumptions for variables and functions. We could keep a separate environment for functions as we did for SFUN, but since terms in FUN may contain local functions, we will need to update the assumptions of types for functions during the typing of the term, as we do with variables. For simplicity, we use just one environment. Moreover, since the language is higher-order and operators can be used in a Curryfied way, we will assume that the environment contains also type information for arithmetic and boolean operators; that is, Γ contains declarations of the form $f_i : \tau$ for global functions, op: τ for boolean and integer operations, x: τ for variables, and f: τ for local functions.

The structure of the environment Γ becomes important now, because we might have several local definitions for an identifier. Therefore Γ will be treated as a stack. We will write

$$\Gamma, \mathsf{id}\colon \tau$$

for the stack obtained by pushing id: τ onto Γ, that is, we represent the top of the stack at the right. We will write $\Gamma(\mathsf{id})$ to denote the rightmost declaration for id in Γ. Formally:

$\Gamma(\mathsf{id}) = \tau$ *if and only if* $\Gamma = \Gamma_1, \mathsf{id}\colon \tau, \Gamma_2$ *and* Γ_2 *does not contain a declaration for* id.

The axioms and rules in Figure 5.3 define the typing relation in **FUN**.

The axiom (**id**) and the rules (**let**) and (**letfun**) deserve some explanations.

We have replaced the axiom (**var**) in the type system of **SFUN** (see Figure 5.1) with a more general axiom that allows us to extract information from the environment in order to assign a type to a variable, a local or global function, or a primitive operator.

In the rule (**let**) we see that Γ has to be treated as a stack rather than a set: we can have nested definitions for the same identifier, in which case Γ will contain several declarations for the same variable. Also note that we type t_1 in the environment Γ, and t_2 in Γ augmented with x: σ since t_2 may contain occurrences of the newly defined local variable x, but t_1 cannot (the `let` construct is not recursive).

The rule (**letfun**) allows us to type recursive functions: we type t_1 in an environment containing type information for the formal arguments $x_1, \ldots,$ x_n and for the newly defined function f. In t_2 we can use f but not the formal arguments.

The rules (**op**), (**bop**), (**and**), (**not**) are no longer needed, because we can type expressions containing operators using (**Ap**) and the information provided in the environment (recall that Γ now contains type assumptions for functions and primitive operators). However, we prefer to include these rules in the type system to simplify the typing of arithmetic and boolean expressions.

We now give some examples of typeable terms in **FUN**.

Example 51 (Typing Terms in FUN) *We will show that the term*

`let fun` *square* x: int $= (x * x)$: int `in` (*square* 3) $+$ (*square* 2)

Axioms:

$$\frac{}{\Gamma \vdash b : \mathsf{bool}} \ (b) \qquad \frac{}{\Gamma \vdash n : \mathsf{int}} \ (n) \qquad \frac{}{\Gamma \vdash \mathit{id} : \sigma} \ (\mathsf{id}) \quad \text{where } \sigma = \Gamma(\mathsf{id})$$

Rules:

$$\frac{\Gamma \vdash t_1 : \mathsf{int} \quad \Gamma \vdash t_2 : \mathsf{int}}{\Gamma \vdash t_1 \ op \ t_2 : \mathsf{int}} \ (\mathsf{op})$$

$$\frac{\Gamma \vdash t_1 : \mathsf{int} \quad \Gamma \vdash t_2 : \mathsf{int}}{\Gamma \vdash t_1 \ bop \ t_2 : \mathsf{bool}} \ (\mathsf{bop})$$

$$\frac{\Gamma \vdash t_1 : \mathsf{bool} \quad \Gamma \vdash t_2 : \mathsf{bool}}{\Gamma \vdash t_1 \wedge t_2 : \mathsf{bool}} \ (\mathsf{and}) \qquad \frac{\Gamma \vdash t : \mathsf{bool}}{\Gamma \vdash \neg t : \mathsf{bool}} \ (\mathsf{not})$$

$$\frac{\Gamma \vdash t_0 : \mathsf{bool} \quad \Gamma \vdash t_1 : \sigma \quad \Gamma \vdash t_2 : \sigma}{\Gamma \vdash \mathsf{if} \ t_0 \ \mathsf{then} \ t_1 \ \mathsf{else} \ t_2 : \sigma} \ (\mathsf{if})$$

$$\frac{\Gamma \vdash t_1 : \sigma \to \tau \quad \Gamma \vdash t_2 : \sigma}{\Gamma \vdash (t_1 \ t_2) : \tau} \ (\mathsf{Ap})$$

$$\frac{\Gamma \vdash t_1 : \sigma \quad \Gamma, x : \sigma \vdash t_2 : \tau}{\Gamma \vdash \mathsf{let} \ x = t_1 \ \mathsf{in} \ t_2 : \tau} \ (\mathsf{let})$$

$$\frac{\Gamma, x_1 : \sigma_1, \dots, x_n : \sigma_n, f : \rho \vdash t_1 : \sigma \quad \Gamma, f : \rho \vdash t_2 : \tau}{\Gamma \vdash \mathsf{let \ fun} \ f \ x_1 : \sigma_2 \ \dots x_n : \sigma_n = t_1 : \sigma \ \mathsf{in} \ t_2 : \tau} \ (\mathsf{letfun})$$
$$\text{where} \quad \rho = \sigma_1 \to \dots \to \sigma_n \to \sigma$$

Figure 5.3: Type System for **FUN**

has type int. *In the type derivations below,* Γ *represents an environment containing the declaration* square: int $\to$ int.

First we show that (square 3) *has type* int, *as follows:*

$$\frac{\dfrac{}{\Gamma \vdash square: \text{int} \to \text{int}} \text{(id)} \quad \dfrac{}{\Gamma \vdash 3: \text{int}} \text{(n)}}{\Gamma \vdash (square\ 3): \text{int}} \text{(Ap)}$$

In the same way we can show $\Gamma \vdash (square\ 2)$: int, *and using rule* (op) *we derive:*

$$\frac{\Gamma \vdash (square\ 3): \text{int} \quad \Gamma \vdash (square\ 2): \text{int}}{\Gamma \vdash (square\ 3) + (square\ 2): \text{int}} \text{(op)}$$

We can also derive the type int *for* $x * x$ *assuming* $\Gamma'(x) = \text{int}$:

$$\frac{\dfrac{}{\Gamma' \vdash x: \text{int}} \text{(id)} \quad \dfrac{}{\Gamma' \vdash x: \text{int}} \text{(id)}}{\Gamma' \vdash (x * x): \text{int}} \text{(op)}$$

Therefore we can use the rule (letfun), *where* Γ' *is the environment* x: int, square: int $\to$ int.

$$\frac{\Gamma' \vdash (x * x): \text{int} \quad \Gamma \vdash (square\ 3) + (square\ 2): \text{int}}{\vdash \texttt{let fun}\ square\ x: \text{int} = (x * x): \text{int}\ \texttt{in}\ (square\ 3) + (square\ 2):\text{int}} \text{(letfun)}$$

Note that the type of the let fun *expression is not necessarily the type of the image of the local function that is being defined. For instance, we can show that the term*

$$\texttt{let fun}\ square\ x: \text{int} = (x * x): \text{int}\ \texttt{in}\ (square\ 3) > (square\ 2)$$

has type bool.

To type check a **FUN** program

$$f_1\ x_1 \ldots x_{a_1} \quad = \quad t_1$$
$$\vdots$$
$$f_k\ x_1 \ldots x_{a_k} \quad = \quad t_k$$

we use the type information provided by the programmer for the global functions $f_1, \ldots, f_k$, in the same way as we did for **SFUN**. Let Γ be an environment containing a type declaration for each global function; assume that for f_i we have $\Gamma(f_i) = \sigma_1 \to \ldots \to \sigma_{a_i} \to \tau_i$. We say that the program is correctly typed if for each equation $f_i\, x_1 \ldots x_{a_i} = t_i$ we have

$$\Gamma, x_1\colon\sigma_1, \ldots, x_{a_i}\colon\sigma_{a_i} \vdash t_i\colon\tau_i$$

In other words, a **FUN** program is well typed if the equations are compatible with the types declared by the programmer for the global functions. The term t_i in the right hand side of the ith equation should have the type of $f_i\, x_1 \ldots x_{a_i}$, that is, τ_i. Note that a_i may be 0, and in contrast with **SFUN**, here τ_i may be any type, for instance it could be an arrow type if the result of f_i is a function. To type the term t_i we use the type system given in Figure 5.3.

We now give examples of programs that are well typed.

Example 52 *Consider the program P defining a global function f_1 as follows:*

$$f_1\, x = \texttt{let } y = (x * x) \texttt{ in } (y * y)$$

and assume $\Gamma(f_1) = \texttt{int} \to \texttt{int}$.

The program P is correctly typed, because $\texttt{let } y = (x * x) \texttt{ in } (y * y)$ *has type* $\texttt{int}$ *in the environment* $\Gamma, x\colon\texttt{int}$, *as the following type derivation shows. The environment* Γ' *is* $\Gamma, x\colon\texttt{int}, y\colon\texttt{int}$.

$$\dfrac{\dfrac{\Gamma, x\colon\texttt{int} \vdash x\colon\texttt{int} \quad \Gamma, x\colon\texttt{int} \vdash x\colon\texttt{int}}{\Gamma, x\colon\texttt{int} \vdash (x * x)\colon\texttt{int}}(\text{op}) \quad \dfrac{\Gamma' \vdash y\colon\texttt{int} \quad \Gamma' \vdash y\colon\texttt{int}}{\Gamma' \vdash (y * y)\colon\texttt{int}}(\text{op})}{\Gamma, x\colon\texttt{int} \vdash \texttt{let } y = (x * x) \texttt{ in } (y * y)\colon\texttt{int}}(\text{let})$$

Note that the program

$$f_1\, x = \texttt{let } x = (x * x) \texttt{ in } (x * x)$$

is also well typed, although less readable.

Consider now the program

$$succ = +\,1$$

which is an example of a program defining a higher-order function. This program is typeable in an environment Γ such that $\Gamma(succ) = \texttt{int} \to \texttt{int}$, and $\Gamma(+) = \texttt{int} \to \texttt{int} \to \texttt{int}$. To show this, we build a type derivation for $\Gamma \vdash +\,1\colon\texttt{int} \to \texttt{int}$.

$$\dfrac{\dfrac{}{\Gamma \vdash +\colon\texttt{int} \to \texttt{int} \to \texttt{int}}(\text{id}) \quad \dfrac{}{\Gamma \vdash 1\colon\texttt{int}}(\text{n})}{\Gamma \vdash +\,1\colon\texttt{int} \to \texttt{int}}(\text{Ap})$$

5.4.3 Operational Semantics of FUN (†)

We will now give a meaning to FUN programs and terms using a transition system. We will define a call-by-value evaluation relation, which we denote by $\Downarrow_P$ to emphasise the fact that the value of a term depends on a given program P. A call-by-name semantics can be obtained by a simple modification of the rules defining $\Downarrow_P$, we will leave it as an exercise.

In order to take into account the local definitions that might occur in FUN terms, we will define $\Downarrow_P$ as a ternary relation between:

- An environment Γ which maps identifiers to values and stores local function definitions. Γ will be represented as a list of pairs, which can be of the form $id = v$ (an identifier and a value), or $f\, x_1 \ldots x_n = t$ (a function definition).

- A well-typed FUN term, which may contain local definitions. All type declarations are erased from the `let fun` constructs before the evaluation: we assume the term is well-typed, but we do not need to know its type to evaluate it.

- A value. Since FUN is a higher-order language, values are integers, booleans and irreducible functions.

We write $\Gamma \vdash t \Downarrow_P v$ to indicate that the term t has the value v in the context of the program P under the assumptions in Γ.

Again, Γ will be structured as a stack, and we will write

$$\Gamma, u = w$$

to denote the stack obtained by pushing the pair $u = w$ onto Γ, that is, the top of the stack is the rightmost pair. The notation $\Gamma(x)$ will be used to extract from Γ the last value associated to x (i.e. the value v in the rightmost pair $x = v$). Similarly, $\Gamma(f\, x_1 \ldots x_n)$ will denote the term t associated to $f\, x_1 \ldots x_n$ in the last definition of the function f.

In Figure 5.4 we give an inductive definition, using a set of axioms and rules, of the evaluation relation $\Downarrow_P$. Some explanations are in order:

FUN constants (integers and booleans) are already values as the axioms (n) and (b) indicate, and so are functions whose arity is greater than 0 and operators: the axiom (fnVal) indicates that FUN is a higher-order language, in contrast with SFUN.

We need an axiom for identifiers (which was not present in the system given for SFUN, see Figure 5.2) in order to extract from the environment Γ the values stored for locally defined variables.

$$\frac{}{\Gamma \vdash n \Downarrow_P n} \text{ (n)} \qquad \frac{}{\Gamma \vdash b \Downarrow_P b} \text{ (b)} \qquad \frac{}{\Gamma \vdash f \Downarrow_P f \quad \text{if } ar(f) > 0} \text{ (fnVal)}$$

$$\frac{}{\Gamma \vdash x \Downarrow_P v \quad \text{if } \Gamma(x) = v} \text{ (id)}$$

$$\frac{\Gamma \vdash t_1 \Downarrow_P n_1 \quad \Gamma \vdash t_2 \Downarrow_P n_2}{\Gamma \vdash t_1 \, op \, t_2 \Downarrow_P n \quad \text{if } n = n_1 \, op \, n_2} \text{ (op)}$$

$$\frac{\Gamma \vdash t_1 \Downarrow_P n_1 \quad \Gamma \vdash t_2 \Downarrow_P n_2}{\Gamma \vdash t_1 \, bop \, t_2 \Downarrow_P b \quad \text{if } b = n_1 \, bop \, n_2} \text{ (bop)}$$

$$\frac{\Gamma \vdash t_1 \Downarrow_P b_1 \quad \Gamma \vdash t_2 \Downarrow_P b_2}{\Gamma \vdash t_1 \wedge t_2 \Downarrow_P b \quad \text{if } b = b_1 \, and \, b_2} \text{ (and)} \qquad \frac{\Gamma \vdash t \Downarrow_P b}{\Gamma \vdash \neg t \Downarrow_P b' \quad \text{if } b' = not \, b} \text{ (not)}$$

$$\frac{\Gamma \vdash t_0 \Downarrow_P True \quad \Gamma \vdash t_1 \Downarrow_P v_1}{\Gamma \vdash \text{if } t_0 \text{ then } t_1 \text{ else } t_2 \Downarrow_P v_1} \text{ (If}_\mathsf{T})$$

$$\frac{\Gamma \vdash t_0 \Downarrow_P False \quad \Gamma \vdash t_2 \Downarrow_P v_2}{\Gamma \vdash \text{if } t_0 \text{ then } t_1 \text{ else } t_2 \Downarrow_P v_2} \text{ (If}_\mathsf{F})$$

$$\frac{\Gamma \vdash t_1 \Downarrow_P v_1 \quad \Gamma, x = v_1 \vdash t_2 \Downarrow_P v}{\Gamma \vdash \text{let } x = t_1 \text{ in } t_2 \Downarrow_P v} \text{ (let)}$$

$$\frac{\Gamma, f \, x_1 \ldots x_n = t_1 \vdash t_2 \Downarrow_P v}{\Gamma \vdash \text{let fun } f \, x_1 \ldots x_n = t_1 \text{ in } t_2 \Downarrow_P v} \text{ (letfun)}$$

$$\frac{\Gamma \vdash s \Downarrow_P (f \, t_1 \ldots t_i) \quad \Gamma \vdash t \Downarrow_P v}{\Gamma \vdash (s \, t) \Downarrow_P (f \, t_1 \ldots t_i \, v) \quad \text{if } ar(f) > i + 1} \text{ (Ap)}$$

$$\frac{\Gamma \vdash s \Downarrow_P f_i \, v_1 \ldots v_{a_i-1} \quad \Gamma \vdash t \Downarrow_P v_{a_i} \quad \Gamma \vdash d_i\{\overline{x_j \mapsto v_j}\} \Downarrow_P v}{\Gamma \vdash (s \, t) \Downarrow_P v \quad \text{if } d_i = def(f_i \, x_1 \ldots x_{a_i})} \text{ (fn)}$$

$$\frac{\Gamma \vdash d_i \Downarrow_P v}{\Gamma \vdash f_i \Downarrow_P v \quad \text{if } d_i = def(f_i)} \text{ (fn0)}$$

Figure 5.4: Call-by-Value Evaluation in **FUN**

The rules for arithmetic and boolean operators are standard, and we have two rules for the if-then-else, as usual.

In the rule (let) we see that Γ has to be treated as a stack: we may have nested evaluations for the same identifier, in which case Γ will contain several values for the same variable. Also note that we evaluate t_1 in the environment Γ, and t_2 in Γ augmented with $x = v_1$ since t_2 may contain occurrences of the new variable x, but t_1 cannot (the let construct is not recursive).

In the rule (letfun) we evaluate t_2 in an environment in which the function f is associated with its last definition.

The rules (Ap) and (fn) deal with applications. (Ap) is used to collect and evaluate the arguments of Curryfied functions (local and global) and operators. If the number of arguments that we have is smaller than the arity of the function we cannot apply it; in this case we just evaluate the arguments and return the application. If all the arguments are provided, the definition of the function, denoted $\text{def}(f_i\, x_1 \ldots x_{a_i})$, is used after all the arguments are evaluated in rule (fn). We have to specify how the definition of the function is obtained:

$$\text{def}(f_i\, x_1 \ldots x_{a_i}) = \begin{cases} \Gamma(f_i\, x_1 \ldots x_{a_i}) & \text{if } f_i \in dom(\Gamma) \\[2mm] d_i & \text{if } f_i \notin dom(\Gamma) \text{ and} \\ & f_i\, x_1 \ldots x_{a_i} = d_i \text{ is in } P \\[2mm] x_1\, f_i\, x_2 & \text{if } f_i \text{ is an arithmetic or} \\ & \text{boolean operator} \end{cases}$$

In other words, we search for the definition of the function f_i first in the environment Γ and then in the program P (i.e. local definitions have priority over global ones); for arithmetic and boolean operators we have ad-hoc evaluation rules.

The notation $d_i\{\overline{x_j \mapsto v_j}\}$ used in rule (fn) is shorthand for

$$d_i\{x_1 \mapsto v_1, \ldots, x_{a_i} \mapsto v_{a_i}\}$$

which represents as usual the term obtained after replacing (simultaneously) in d_i each occurrence of x_1 by v_1, x_2 by v_2, etc.

Rule (fn0) deals with the special case of 0-ary functions, for which we do not need to evaluate any arguments. In this case, $\text{def}(f_i) = \Gamma(f_i)$ if f_i is a locally defined function, otherwise, if $f_i = d_i$ is in P, $\text{def}(f_i) = d_i$.

Again, we observe that the system is syntax-directed: given a term to evaluate (i.e. a labelled syntax tree), the labels in the tree indicate the rules or axioms that should be applied.

We end this section with some examples of evaluation.

Example 53 *We can show that the term*

$$\texttt{let fun } square\ x\text{:}\ \textsf{int} = (x * x)\text{:}\ \textsf{int in } (square\ 3) + (square\ 2)$$

has the value 13 (independently of the given program P) as follows.

First we show that (square 3) has the value 9 in an environment Γ that contains the definition $square\ x = x * x$ (i.e. $\Gamma(square\ x) = x * x$). We omit the derivation of $\Gamma \vdash 3 * 3 \Downarrow_P 9$.

$$\cfrac{\cfrac{}{\Gamma \vdash square \Downarrow_P square}\ (\textsf{fnVal}) \qquad \cfrac{}{\Gamma \vdash 3 \Downarrow_P 3}\ (\textsf{n}) \qquad \Gamma \vdash 3 * 3 \Downarrow_P 9}{\Gamma \vdash (square\ 3) \Downarrow_P 9}\ (\textsf{fn})$$

In the same way we can show $\Gamma \vdash (square\ 2) \Downarrow_P 4$.

We use these derivations below, where again Γ is the environment containing the definition $square\ x = x * x$. Note that we evaluate the term obtained after erasing all type-annotations.

$$\cfrac{\cfrac{\Gamma \vdash (square\ 3) \Downarrow_P 9 \quad \Gamma \vdash (square\ 2) \Downarrow_P 4}{\Gamma \vdash (square\ 3) + (square\ 2) \Downarrow_P 13}\ (\textsf{op})}{\vdash \texttt{let fun } square\ x = x * x \texttt{ in } (square\ 3) + (square\ 2) \Downarrow_P 13}\ (\textsf{letfun})$$

Consider now the program P defining the higher-order (0-ary) function succ:

$$succ = +\,1$$

We can show that the term (succ 3) evaluates to 4 as follows (we omit the derivation for $\vdash 1 + 3 \Downarrow_P 4$).

$$\cfrac{\cfrac{\cfrac{\cfrac{}{\vdash + \Downarrow_P +}\ (\textsf{fnVal}) \quad \cfrac{}{\vdash 1 \Downarrow_P 1}\ (\textsf{n})}{\vdash +\,1 \Downarrow_P +\,1}\ (\textsf{Ap})}{\vdash succ \Downarrow_P +\,1}\ (\textsf{fn0}) \quad \cfrac{}{\vdash 3 \Downarrow_P 3}\ (\textsf{n}) \quad \vdash 1 + 3 \Downarrow_P 4}{\vdash (succ\ 3) \Downarrow_P 4}\ (\textsf{fn})$$

5.4.4 Properties of FUN (†)

The language FUN with the type system and the semantics defined above is not strongly typed. We can give examples of correctly typed terms which fail to produce a value.

Example 54 *Consider the term:*

```
let    x = 0    in
       let fun   f y: int = (x + y): int  in
              let  x = True  in  (f 3)
```

To see that this is a typeable term:

First we show that $\Gamma' \vdash$ let $x = True$ in $(f\ 3) :$ int, *where* Γ' *is the type environment* $x:$ int, $f:$ int $\rightarrow$ int.

$$
\cfrac{
\cfrac{}{\Gamma' \vdash True:\text{bool}}\ (b) \quad
\cfrac{
\cfrac{}{\Gamma', x:\text{bool} \vdash f:\text{int} \rightarrow \text{int}}\ (id) \quad
\cfrac{}{\vdash 3:\text{int}}\ (n)
}{
\cfrac{\Gamma', x:\text{bool} \vdash (f\ 3):\text{int}}{}
}\ (Ap)
}{
\Gamma' \vdash \text{let } x = True \text{ in } (f\ 3) : \text{int}
}\ (let)
$$

Using the type derivation above, we can show that our original term has type int. *Below,* Γ *is the type environment* $x:$ int, $y:$ int, $f:$ int $\rightarrow$ int, *and* t *represents the term* let $x = True$ in $(f\ 3)$.

$$
\cfrac{
\cfrac{}{\vdash 0:\text{int}}\ (n) \quad
\cfrac{
\cfrac{
\cfrac{}{\Gamma \vdash x:\text{int}}\ (id) \quad \cfrac{}{\Gamma \vdash y:\text{int}}\ (id)
}{\Gamma \vdash x + y:\text{int}}\ (op) \quad \Gamma' \vdash t : \text{int}
}{x:\text{int} \vdash \text{let fun } f\ y:\text{int} = (x + y):\text{int in } t : \text{int}}\ (letfun)
}{
\vdash \text{let } x = 0 \text{ in let fun } f\ y:\text{int} = (x + y):\text{int in } t : \text{int}
}\ (let)
$$

Now, during the evaluation of this term according to the semantics of FUN *we reach a point in which we have to obtain a value for* $(f\ 3)$ *in an evaluation environment* Γ' *where* $x = True$. *We show the derivation below.* Γ *represents the evaluation context* $x = 0, f\ y = x + y$, *and* Γ' *represents* $x = 0, f\ y = x + y, x = True$. *As before the term* t *represents* let $x = True$ in $(f\ 3)$.

$$
\cfrac{
\cfrac{}{\vdash 0 \Downarrow_P 0}\ (n) \quad
\cfrac{
\cfrac{
\cfrac{}{\Gamma \vdash True \Downarrow_P True}\ (b) \quad \Gamma' \vdash (f\ 3) \Downarrow_P ?
}{\Gamma \vdash t \Downarrow_P ?}\ (let)
}{x = 0 \vdash \text{let fun } f\ y = (x + y) \text{ in } t \Downarrow_P ?}\ (letfun)
}{
\vdash \text{let } x = 0 \text{ in let fun } f\ y = x + y \text{ in } t \Downarrow_P ?
}\ (let)
$$

Therefore to complete the evaluation we must derive a value for $(f\ 3)$ *in* Γ'. *The only evaluation rule that can be applied is* (fn), *but it requires the* *evaluation of $x + 3$ in Γ':*

$$\frac{\overline{\Gamma' \vdash f \Downarrow_P f} \text{ (fnVal)} \quad \overline{\Gamma' \vdash 3 \Downarrow_P 3} \text{ (n)} \quad \Gamma' \vdash x + 3 \Downarrow_P?}{\Gamma' \vdash (f\ 3) \Downarrow_P?} \text{ (fn)}$$

Only one rule can apply to $x + 3$: we must use (op). *But when we try to add True and 3 a type error arises.*

$$\frac{\overline{\Gamma' \vdash x \Downarrow_P True} \text{ (id)} \quad \overline{\Gamma' \vdash 3 \Downarrow_P 3} \text{ (n)}}{\Gamma' \vdash x + 3 \Downarrow_P?} \text{ (op)}$$

The problem is that our evaluation rules for local definitions specify a *dynamic binding* for identifiers, as the previous example shows. More precisely, in the evaluation of the term $(f\ 3)$, where $f\ y = x + y$, the value of x is the one available at the calling point, rather than the one available when the function f was defined (see Chapter 2 for a discussion and examples of static and dynamic binding).

To obtain a semantics with static binding, in rule (letfun) we should store in the evaluation environment not only the body of the function but also the current environment. A functional value should also be represented as a pair, including an environment. We leave this as an exercise for the interested readers.

5.5   Exercises

1. Write a SFUN program defining the functions min and max that take a pair of numbers as arguments and compute the minimum and maximum respectively.

2. Write a SFUN program defining a function fibonacci that takes a natural number n as argument and produces the nth Fibonacci number as a result (see Exercise 1 in Chapter 4).

3. Show that the SFUN program

$$\begin{aligned} square(x) &= x * x \\ double(x) &= 2 * x \end{aligned}$$

and the term $square(double(3))$ are well-typed in an environment ε such that

$\varepsilon(square) = \text{int} \rightarrow \text{int}$

$\varepsilon(double) = \text{int} \rightarrow \text{int}$

4. Show the evaluation of the SFUN term $square(double(3))$ with respect to the program:

$$square(x) \quad = \quad x * x$$
$$double(x) \quad = \quad 2 * x$$

using first the call-by-value semantics, then the call-by-name semantics.

5. Give more examples of programs in SFUN that have different results under call-by-value and call-by-name.

6. Prove the Unicity of Types in SFUN, that is, show that for any SFUN term t, if $\Gamma \vdash_\varepsilon t : \sigma$ and $\Gamma \vdash_\varepsilon t : \tau$ then $\sigma = \tau$.

7. (†) Prove the following substitution lemma:

   If $x_1 : \sigma_1, \ldots, x_n : \sigma_n \vdash_\varepsilon t : \tau$ and $t_1, \ldots, t_n$ are closed terms such that $\vdash_\varepsilon t_i : \sigma_i$ for $1 \leq i \leq n$, then $\vdash_\varepsilon t\{x_i \mapsto t_i\} : \tau$.

   Using this result and the call-by-value semantics of the language SFUN, show that the evaluation relation preserves types. That is, if P is a SFUN program which is typeable in an environment ε, and t is a closed term, then the following property holds: If $t \Downarrow_P^V v$ and $\Gamma \vdash_\varepsilon t : \tau$ then $\Gamma \vdash_\varepsilon v : \tau$.

8. Explain what the following FUN functions do

$$f_1\, x = \texttt{let } y = x * x \texttt{ in } y * y$$

$$f_2\, x = \texttt{let } x = x * x \texttt{ in } x * x$$

   Show that this program is typeable in an environment Γ where

$$\Gamma(f_1) = \Gamma(f_2) = \text{int} \to \text{int}$$

9. Show that the FUN term

   $\texttt{let fun } square\ x : \text{int} = (x * x) : \text{int} \texttt{ in } (square\ 3) > (square\ 2)$

   has type bool, and derive its value using the semantics of FUN (Figure 5.4).

10. (†) Give a call-by-name semantics for FUN.

11. (†) Modify the evaluation rules defining the semantics of FUN in order to obtain a version of the language with static binding.

Part III

Logic Languages

Chapter 6

Logic Programming Languages

We have already discussed two approaches to programming: the imperative and the functional paradigms. If we had to single out one major difference between functional and imperative programs, we could perhaps say that functional programs are concerned with *what* needs to be computed whereas imperative programs indicate *how* to compute it: functional languages are *declarative*. There is another interesting family of declarative languages, which has its roots in logic: *logic programming languages*.

Roughly speaking, programs in logic programming languages are logical formulas describing a problem, and the execution of a program is a process of proof searching during which solutions for the problem will be generated. Since programs are just descriptions of problems, this is a knowledge-based programming style which has many applications in artificial intelligence (for example, to build expert systems).

The language of logic is a very powerful one. The same formalism can be used to specify a problem, write a program, and prove properties of the program. The same program can be used in many different ways. Based on this idea, several programming languages have been developed which differ in the kind of logic that is used for the description of the problem and the method employed to find proofs. The most well-known logic programming language is *Prolog*, which is based on first-order predicate calculus and uses the Principle of Resolution [17]. Actually, first-order logic and the Resolution Principle are too general to be used directly as a programming language, but in the 70's R. Kowalski, A. Colmerauer and P. Roussel defined and implemented a suitable restriction, based on the clausal fragment of classical first-order logic, which resulted in the first version of Prolog [18].

Nowadays, several versions of Prolog exist. The basic framework has been enriched to make it more efficient and easier to use. Extensions include primitive data types such as integers and real numbers, advanced optimisation techniques, file-handling facilities, graphical interfaces, control mechanisms, etc. Some of these features are non-declarative, and often programs that use them are called *impure* because, to achieve efficiency, in the program the problem description is mixed with implementation details (i.e. the *what* and the *how* are mixed). Constraint logic programming languages, which were developed from Prolog, achieve efficiency by incorporating optimised proof search methods for specific domains.

In this book we will only consider the pure fragment of Prolog. We will see how logic can be used to express knowledge and describe problems, and how this knowledge or problem description can be manipulated to compute solutions to a problem, using Resolution as inference rule.

In this chapter we give an overview of the logic programming paradigm: we start by defining the domain of computation of logic programs, then we describe how programs are built, and how they are used. We study the operational semantics of Prolog in Chapter 7.

For the examples in this part of the book we will use a generic notation inspired by the syntax of SWI-Prolog, a free Prolog compiler which can be downloaded together with the reference manual from `www.swi-prolog.org`.

6.1   The Herbrand Universe

The domain of computation of logic programs is the *Herbrand Universe*, named after Jacques Herbrand, a French mathematician who studied logical deduction as a computation mechanism in the 30's.

The Herbrand Universe is the set of *terms* defined over a universal *alphabet* of

- *variables*, such as X, Y, etc

- and *function symbols* with fixed arities (the arity of a symbol is as usual the number of arguments associated with it).

  Function symbols are denoted by f, g, h, or a, b, c if the arity is 0 (constants).

Definition 55 *A* term *is either a variable, or has the form* $f(t_1, \ldots, t_n)$ *where* f *is a function symbol of arity* n *and* $t_1, \ldots, t_n$ *are terms.*

Example 56 *If a is a constant, f a binary function, and g a unary function, then $f(f(X, g(a)), Y)$ is a term, where X, Y are variables.*

Function symbols in logic programs correspond to the constructors used to define data in functional languages. They are used to give structure to the domain of computation. There is no definition associated to a function symbol in a logic program (except for some built-in functions, such as arithmetic operations, which have a specific meaning).

In logic programming languages no specific alphabet is assumed, the programmer can freely choose the names of variables and functions needed to represent the problem domain. However, Prolog's syntax requires that names of variables start with capital letters and names of functions start with lower-case. Also, function names should be different from built-in operations.

6.2 Logic Programs

Once the domain of computation is established, the problem can be described by means of logic formulas involving *predicates*.

Predicates represent properties of terms, and are used to build basic formulas which are then composed using operators such as *and, not, implies*.

Definition 57 *Let $\mathcal{P}$ be a set of* predicate symbols, *each with a fixed arity. If p is a predicate of arity n and $t_1, \ldots, t_n$ are terms, then $p(t_1, \ldots, t_n)$ is an* atomic formula, *or simply an* atom. *A* literal *is an atomic formula or a negated atomic formula.*

We give now some examples of atoms that can appear in logic programs.

Example 58 *The following are two literals, where we use the predicates* valueSIMP *of arity 2 and* raining *of arity 0, a unary function symbol* number, *and the constant 1:*

```
valueSIMP(number(1),1)
¬raining
```

We have followed another syntactic convention of Prolog: names of predicates start with lower-case.

Definition 59 (Programs) *Prolog programs are sets of* definite clauses, *also called* Horn clauses, *which are a restricted class of first-order formulas. A* definite clause *is a disjunction of literals with at most one positive literal.*

We have to introduce more notational conventions:

We write P_1, P_2,... to denote atoms.

A definite clause $P_1 \lor \neg P_2 \lor \ldots \lor \neg P_n$ (where P_1 is the only positive literal) will be written:

$$P_1 \; :\text{-} \; P_2, \ldots, P_n.$$

and we read it as:

$$\text{``}P_1 \text{ if } P_2 \text{ and } \ldots \text{ and } P_n\text{''}$$

We call P_1 the *head* of the clause, and $P_2, \ldots, P_n$ the *body*.

If the clause contains just P_1 and no negative literals, then we write

$$P_1.$$

Both kinds of clauses are called *program clauses*, the first kind is called a *rule* and the second kind is called a *fact*.

If the clause contains only negative literals, we call it a *goal* or *query* and write

$$:\text{-}P_2, \ldots, P_n.$$

Program clauses can be seen as defining a database: facts specify information to be stored and rules indicate how we can deduce more information from the previously defined data.

Goals are questions to be answered using the information about the problem in the database. This can be better seen with some examples.

Example 60 *1. In the following Prolog program the first four clauses are facts and the last one is a rule.*

```
based(prolog,logic).¹
based(haskell,maths).
likes(claire,maths).
likes(max,logic).
likes(X,L) :- based(L,Y), likes(X,Y).
```

We use two binary predicates: based *and* likes, *functional symbols* prolog, logic, haskell, maths, claire, max *of arity 0, and variables* X, Y, L.

---

[1] In some versions of Prolog the word prolog is reserved, therefore to run this example you might need to replace prolog by myprolog for instance.

The first two clauses in the program can be read as "Prolog is based on logic and Haskell on mathematics". More precisely, these are facts about the predicate based, *they define a relation to be stored in the database.*

The next three clauses define the predicate likes. *There are two facts, which can be read as "Claire likes mathematics and Max likes logic", and a rule which allows us to deduce more information about people's tastes: we can read this rule as "X likes L if L is based on Y and X likes Y".*

Once this information is specified in the program as shown above, we can ask questions such as "is there somebody (some Z) who likes Prolog?" which corresponds to the goal:

```
:- likes(Z,prolog).
```

With the information given in the program, we can deduce that Max likes Prolog: we know that Max likes logic and Prolog is based on logic, and therefore the last rule allows us to conclude that Max likes Prolog.

The precise algorithm that Prolog uses to reach this conclusion using resolution as inference rule will be described in Chapter 7.

2. *We can use arithmetic operations in program clauses. To obtain the value of an arithmetic expression we use the built-in predicate* is. *For instance, we can define the predicate* mean *by*

```
mean(A,B,C) :- C is (A+B)/2.
```

6.3　Finding Answers

Answers to goals will be represented by *substitutions* that associate values to the unknowns (i.e. the variables) in the goal. *Values* are also terms.

Definition 61 (Substitution) *A substitution is a partial mapping from variables to terms, with a finite domain. If the domain of the substitution σ is*

$$dom(\sigma) = \{X_1, \ldots, X_n\}$$

we denote the substitution by: $\{X_1 \mapsto t_1, \ldots, X_n \mapsto t_n\}$.

　　Substitutions are extended to terms and literals as usual: We apply a substitution σ to a term t or a literal l by simultaneously replacing each *variable occurring in dom(σ) by the corresponding term. The resulting term is denoted tσ.*

Since substitutions are functions, composition of substitutions *is simply functional composition. For example, $\sigma \cdot \rho$ denotes the composition of σ and ρ.*

Example 62 *The application of the substitution*

$$\sigma = \{X \mapsto g(Y), Y \mapsto a\}$$

to the term

$$f(f(X, g(a)), Y)$$

yields the term

$$f(f(g(Y), g(a)), a)$$

Note the simultaneous replacement of X and Y in the term above.

The behaviour of logic programs can be described in two ways: there is a *declarative interpretation,* in which the meaning of the program is defined with respect to a mathematical model (the Herbrand Universe), and a *procedural interpretation,* which explains how the program is used in computations. The first corresponds to a *denotational semantics* of programs and the second gives an *operational semantics.*

The operational semantics of Prolog is based on the use of SLD-Resolution, a specific version of the Principle of Resolution which we will describe in Chapter 7. Using SLD-resolution Prolog will consider different alternatives to find a solution for a given goal in the context of a program. These alternatives will be represented as branches in a tree, called the *SLD-resolution* tree, or simply SLD-tree. Some of the branches in the SLD-tree may not produce a solution, and after arriving to the end of such a branch, which is called a *failure,* Prolog will *backtrack* to the nearest point in the tree where there are still alternative branches to explore. It will continue traversing the SLD-tree until all the alternatives are exhausted.

Prolog supports interactive programming: the user can submit a query and ask for the first solution, or for more solutions. Functional programming languages can also work in an interactive mode, but in functional languages the interaction is achieved by submitting expressions to be evaluated using a collection of function definitions and each expression produces at most one result. Instead, in logic languages the interaction is achieved by means of queries that are resolved using a collection of predicate definitions and several answers may be found.

To see the analogy (and the differences) between function definitions and predicate definitions, let us look at a Prolog program defining the predicate append for lists[2]. In Prolog the empty list is denoted [], and a non-empty list is denoted as [X|L] where X represents the first element of the list (also called the *head*) and L is the rest of the list (also called the *tail* of the list). We abbreviate [X|[]] as [X], and [X|[Y|[]]] as [X,Y].

Example 63 *The predicate* append *is defined as a relation between three lists: the two lists we want to concatenate and their concatenation. More precisely, the atomic formula* append(S,T,U) *indicates that the result of appending the list* T *onto the end of list* S *is the list* U*. We can define the predicate* append *in Prolog by giving two program clauses (a fact and a rule):*

```
append([],L,L).
append([X|L],Y,[X|Z]) :- append(L,Y,Z).
```

Now compare with the functional definition of append:

$$append([\,],l) = l$$
$$append(x : l, y) = x : append(l, y)$$

Clauses and equations play similar roles. With both programs we can concatenate lists, for instance, the solution to the goal

```
:- append([0],[1,2],U).
```

is a substitution associating to U *the value* [0,1,2] *as we explain below, and the result of the functional expression* $append([0], [1, 2])$ *is the list* $[0, 1, 2]$*. However, logic programs do not have a fixed input-output semantics:* append *is a relation, and can be used in different ways. For instance, with the same logic program and the goal*

```
:- append([0],U,[0,1,2]).
```

we will obtain the solution U = [1,2]*. In this case, the first and third arguments of the predicate are used as input and the second as output. All combinations are possible.*

Answers to goals (i.e. substitutions mapping variables to values) will be automatically generated by the *unification algorithm* which is part of the process of resolution. When Prolog reads a goal, it will try to find in the program the clauses that can be applied. During this process, some equations between terms will be generated, and the unification algorithm will be

---

[2]The predicate **append** is predefined in most Prolog implementations.

called in order to solve these equations. If there is a solution, there is also one that is the most general solution, in the sense that all the others can be derived from it. This is called the *most general unifier*. We will formally define unification problems and give a unification algorithm in Chapter 7, but we can already give an example.

Example 64 *To solve the query*

```
:- append([0],[1,2],U).
```

in the context of the logic program

```
append([],L,L).
append([X|L],Y,[X|Z]) :- append(L,Y,Z).
```

Prolog will start by using the second program clause (the first one cannot be applied because in our goal the first list is not empty). The substitution

$$\{X \mapsto 0,\ L \mapsto [\,],\ Y \mapsto [1,2],\ U \mapsto [0|Z]\}$$

unifies *the head of the second program clause with the query, that is, if we apply this substitution to the literals*

$$\texttt{append([X|L],Y,[X|Z])} \ and \ \texttt{append([0],[1,2],U)}$$

we obtain exactly the same result: `append([0],[1,2],[0|Z])`.

Since the clause says that `append([X|L],Y,[X|Z])` *holds if* `append(L,Y,Z)` *holds, all that remains to prove is that* `append([],[1,2],Z)` *holds for some Z.*

Now we have an atom in which the first list is empty, and we have a fact `append([],L,L)` *in the program. Applying the substitution*

$$\{Z \mapsto [1,2]\}$$

to our atom, we obtain (an instance of) a fact.

Combining both substitutions we get:

$$\{U \mapsto [0,1,2]\}$$

which solves the query. It is the most general answer substitution for the given goal, and the process by which we derived this solution is an example of application of the Principle of Resolution.

Goals such as:

```
:- append([0],[1,2],U)
:- append(X,[1,2],U)
:- append([1,2], U,[0])
```

can all be seen as questions to be answered using the definitions given in the program. The first one has only one solution:

$$\{U \mapsto [0,1,2]\}$$

The second has an infinite number of solutions, and the third one has none.

We refer the reader to [4] for more examples of logic programs. In the following chapter we will study in more detail the operational semantics of Prolog.

6.4 Exercises

1. Assuming that A, B, C are atoms, which of the following clauses are Horn clauses:

    (a) $\neg A$

    (b) $A \lor B \lor \neg C$

    (c) $A \lor \neg A$

    (d) A

2. Test the program:

    ```
    based(myprolog,logic).
    based(haskell,maths).
    likes(claire,maths).
    likes(max,logic).
    likes(X,L) :- based(L,Y), likes(X,Y).
    ```

    with the goals:

    ```
    :- likes(Z,myprolog).
    :- likes(X,maths).
    :- likes(max,X).
    ```

Type n in SWI-Prolog to obtain the next answer for a goal with more than one answer.

3. Numbers and arithmetic operations are predefined in Prolog. Assume we define the predicate `mean` using the clause:

```
mean(A,B,C) :- C is (A+B)/2.
```

What are the answers to the following goals:

```
:- mean(2,4,X).
:- mean(2,4,6).
```

4. Lists are also predefined in Prolog. In particular the predicate `append` is predefined, but in this exercise we will define a new append:

```
myappend([],Y,Y).
myappend([H|T],Y,[H|U]) :- myappend(T,Y,U).
```

What are the answers to the following goals?

```
:- myappend([1,2],[3,4,5],[1,2,3,4,5]).
:- myappend([1,2],[3,4,5],[1,2]).
:- myappend([1,2],[3,4,5],X).
:- myappend([1,2],X,[1,2,3,4,5]).
:- myappend(X,[3,4,5],[1,2,3,4,5]).
:- myappend(X,Y,[1,2,3,4,5]).
:- myappend(X,Y,Z).
```

Explain the answers.

5. Change the order of the clauses in the previous program, and try to explain the behaviour of the new program.

Chapter 7

Operational Semantics of Prolog

In this chapter we will describe the operational interpretation of Prolog programs. More precisely, we will describe how a Prolog interpreter proceeds to solve goals in the context of a given program.

We have already mentioned in the previous chapter that Prolog is based on the Resolution Principle. We will start by defining unification, which is a key step in the Principle of Resolution. Then we will define SLD-resolution, which is the version of resolution used in Prolog, and we will see how Prolog traverses the SLD-tree to find solutions for goals.

7.1   Unification

The unification algorithm was sketched by J. Herbrand in his thesis in the 30's. Later, A. Robinson introduced the Principle of Resolution and gave an algorithm to unify terms, which was the basis for the implementation of Prolog. The version of the unification algorithm that we present is based on the work of M. Martelli and U. Montanari [7].

A *unification problem* $\mathcal{U}$ is a set of equations between terms containing variables. We will use the notation:

$$\{s_1 = t_1, \ldots, s_n = t_n\}$$

A solution to $\mathcal{U}$, also called a *unifier*, is a substitution σ (see Definition 61 in Chapter 6) such that when we apply σ to all the terms in the equations in $\mathcal{U}$ we obtain syntactical identities: for each equation $s_i = t_i$, the terms $s_i\sigma$ and $t_i\sigma$ coincide.

The algorithm of Martelli and Montanari finds the most general unifier for a unification problem if a solution exists, otherwise it fails, indicating that there are no solutions. To find the most general unifier for a unification problem, the algorithm simplifies (i.e. transforms) the set of equations until a substitution is generated.

The way equations are simplified is specified by a set of transformation rules, which apply to sets of equations and produce new sets of equations or a failure.

Unification Algorithm.

Input: A finite set of equations between terms:

$$\{s_1 = t_1, \ldots, s_n = t_n\}$$

Output: A substitution which is the most general unifier for these terms, or failure.

Transformation Rules: The rules that are given below transform a unification problem into a simpler one, or produce a failure. Below E denotes an arbitrary set of equations between terms.

$$(1) \quad f(s_1, \ldots, s_n) = f(t_1, \ldots, t_n), E \quad \rightarrow \quad s_1 = t_1, \ldots, s_n = t_n, E$$

$$(2) \quad f(s_1, \ldots, s_n) = g(t_1, \ldots, t_m), E \quad \rightarrow \quad failure$$

$$(3) \qquad\qquad\qquad X = X, E \quad \rightarrow \quad E$$

$(4) \qquad\qquad\qquad t = X, E \quad \rightarrow \quad X = t, E \qquad$ if t is not a variable

$(5) \qquad\qquad\qquad X = t, E \quad \rightarrow \quad X = t, E\{X \mapsto t\} \quad$ if X is not in t and X occurs in E

$(6) \qquad\qquad\qquad X = t, E \quad \rightarrow \quad failure \quad$ if x occurs in t and $x \neq t$

The unification algorithm applies the transformation rules in a non-deterministic way until no rule can be applied or a failure arises. Note that we are working with *sets* of equations, therefore the order in which they appear in the unification problem is not important.

The test in case (6) is called *occur-check*, for example: $x = f(x)$ fails. This test is time consuming, and for this reason in some systems it is not implemented.

If the algorithm finishes without a failure, by changing in the final set of equations the "=" by $\mapsto$ we obtain a substitution, which is the *most general unifier* (mgu) of the initial set of equations.

Note that rules (1) and (2) apply also to constants (i.e. 0-ary functions): in the first case the equation is deleted and in the second there is a failure.

Example 65   *1. We start with $\{f(a,a) = f(X,a)\}$:*

(a) *using rule (1) this problem rewrites to $\{a = X, a = a\}$,*

(b) *using rule (4) we get $\{X = a, a = a\}$,*

(c) *using rule (1) again we get $\{X = a\}$.*

Now no rule can be applied, therefore the algorithm terminates with the most general unifier $\{X \mapsto a\}$.

2. In Chapter 6, Example 64, we solved the unification problem:

{[X|L] = [0], Y = [1,2], [X|Z] = U}

Recall that [|] is a binary function symbol (a list constructor: its arguments are the head and the tail of the list respectively). [0] is a shorthand for [0|[]], and [] is a constant (the empty list).

We apply the unification algorithm, starting with the above set of equations:

(a) *using rule (1) in the first equation, we get:*
    {X = 0, L = [], Y = [1,2], [X|Z] = U}

(b) *using rule (5) and the first equation we get:*
    {X = 0, L = [], Y = [1,2], [0|Z] = U}

(c) *using rule (4) and the last equation we get:*
    {X = 0, L = [], Y = [1,2], U = [0|Z]}

Then the algorithm stops. Therefore the most general unifier is:
{X $\mapsto$ 0, L $\mapsto$ [],Y $\mapsto$ [1,2], U $\mapsto$ [0|Z]}

7.2   The Principle of Resolution

Resolution is based on *refutation.* In order to solve a query

$$:-\ A_1,\ldots,A_n$$

with respect to a set P of program clauses, resolution seeks to show that

$$P, \neg A_1, \ldots, \neg A_n$$

leads to a contradiction. That is, the negation of the literals in the goal is added to the program P; if a contradiction arises, then we know that P did entail the literals in the query.

Definition 66 *A contradiction is obtained when a literal and its negation are stated at the same time.*

For example: A, $\neg A$ is a contradiction.

If a contradiction does not arise directly from the program and the goal, new clauses will be derived by resolution, and the process will continue until a contradiction arises (the search may continue forever). The derived clauses are called *resolvents.*

We will describe the generation of resolvents using a restriction of the Resolution Principle called SLD-resolution.

7.2.1   SLD-Resolution

Let us consider first a simple case, where in the query there is just one atom. If we have a goal:

$$:-\ \mathsf{a}(u_1,\ldots,u_n)\,.$$

and a program clause (we rename the variables in the clause if necessary so that all the variables are different from those in the goal):

$$\mathsf{a}(t_1,\ldots,t_n)\ :-\ S_1,\ldots,S_m\,.$$

and $\mathsf{a}(t_1,\ldots,t_n)$ and $\mathsf{a}(u_1,\ldots,u_n)$ are unifiable with mgu σ, then we obtain a resolvent:

$$:-\ S_1\sigma,\ldots,S_m\sigma\,.$$

In the general case, the query may have several literals. Prolog's SLD-resolution generates a resolvent using the first one.

Definition 67 (SLD-Resolution) *If the query has several literals, for instance:*

:- $A_1, \ldots, A_k$.

the resolvent *is computed between the* first *atom in the goal (A_1) and a (possibly renamed) program clause. If there is a program clause*

A_1' :- $S_1, \ldots, S_m$.

such that A_1' and A_1 are unifiable with mgu σ, then we obtain a resolvent

:- $S_1\sigma, \ldots, S_m\sigma, A_2\sigma, \ldots, A_k\sigma$.

In other words, the resolvent is generated by replacing the first atom in the goal which unifies with the head of a clause by the body of the clause, and applying the unifier to all the atoms in the new goal.

Note that when we compute a resolvent using a fact (i.e. when $m = 0$), the atom disappears from the query.

An empty resolvent indicates a contradiction, which we will denote by the symbol $\Diamond$.

We stress the fact that each resolution step computes a resolvent between the first atom of the last resolvent obtained and a clause in the program. This is why this particular form of resolution is called *SLD-resolution*:

The 'S' stands for *selection rule*: a fixed computation rule is applied in order to select a particular atom to resolve upon in the goal. Prolog always selects the *leftmost* literal in the goal.

The 'D' stands for *definite*: it indicates that all the program clauses are definite.

The 'L' stands for *linear*, indicating that each resolution step uses the most recent resolvent (to start with, it uses the given query) and a program clause. Prolog uses the clauses in the program *in the order they are written*.

Given a program and a query, the idea is to continue generating resolvents until an empty one (a contradiction) is generated. When an empty resolvent is generated, the composition of all the substitutions applied at each resolution step leading to the contradiction is computed. This is also a substitution (recall that substitutions are functions from terms to terms and composition is functional composition, see Chapter 6 for more details).

The restriction of this substitution to the variables that occur in the initial goal is the *answer* to the initial query.

We represent each resolution step graphically as follows:

$$\begin{array}{c} \text{Query} \\ |\ \textit{mgu} \\ \text{Resolvent} \end{array}$$

Since there might be several clauses in the program that can be used to generate a resolvent for a given query, we obtain a branching structure called *SLD-resolution tree*.

Definition 68 *Every branch in the SLD-tree that leads to an empty resolvent produces an answer. All the branches that produce an answer are called* success branches.

If a finite branch does not lead to an empty resolvent, it is a failure.

An SLD-resolution tree may have several success branches, failure branches, and also infinite branches that arise when we can continue generating resolvents but never reach an empty one.

Example 69 *Consider the program P*

```
based(prolog,logic).
based(haskell,maths).
likes(max,logic).
likes(claire,maths).
likes(X,P) :- based(P,Y), likes(X,Y).
```

and the query

```
:- likes(Z,prolog).
```

Using the last clause, and the mgu $\{X \mapsto Z, P \mapsto \text{prolog}\}$ *we obtain the resolvent*

```
:- based(prolog,Y), likes(Z,Y).
```

Now using the first clause and the mgu $\{Y \mapsto \text{logic}\}$ *we obtain the new resolvent*

```
:- likes(Z,logic).
```

likes(Z,prolog)

| $\{X \mapsto Z, P \mapsto prolog\}$

based(prolog,Y), likes(Z,Y)

| $\{Y \mapsto logic\}$

likes(Z,logic).

$\{Z \mapsto max\}$ / \ $\{X' \mapsto Z, P' \mapsto logic\}$

$\Diamond$ based(logic,Y'),likes(Z,Y')
(Failure)

Figure 7.1: SLD-tree for the query :- likes(Z,prolog). in the context of the program P.

Finally, since we can unify this atom with with the fact likes(max,logic) *using the substitution* $\{Z \mapsto max\}$ *we obtain an empty resolvent. This is therefore a success branch in the SLD-tree for the initial query.*

The composition of the substitutions used in this branch is:

$\{X \mapsto max, P \mapsto prolog, Y \mapsto logic, Z \mapsto max\}$

Therefore, the answer to the initial query is $\{Z \mapsto max\}$.

There are other branches in the SLD-tree for this query, but this is the only successful one. The SLD-resolution tree for this query is shown in Figure 7.1. Note that in the branch that leads to failure we use again the last clause of the program but rename its variables to X', P', Y' *to avoid confusion with the previous use of this clause (see Definition 67).*

Consider now the same program with an additional clause:

likes(claire,logic).

The new program will be called P'.

The SLD-resolution tree for the same query in the context of the program P' *is shown in Figure 7.2.*

likes(Z,prolog)

| $\{X \mapsto Z, \ P \mapsto$ prolog$\}$

based(prolog,Y), likes(Z,Y)

| $\{Y \mapsto$ logic$\}$

likes(Z,logic).

$\{Z \mapsto$ max$\}/$ $\{Z \mapsto$ claire$\}|$ \

◊   ◊   based(logic,Y'),likes(Z,Y')
                                      (Failure)

Figure 7.2: SLD-tree for :- likes(Z,prolog). in the context of P'.

Finally, with the same program and a query

:- likes(Z,painting).

the SLD-tree is:

likes(Z,painting)

| $\{X \mapsto Z, \ P \mapsto$ painting$\}$

based(painting,Y), likes(Z,Y)
(Failure)

7.3 Prolog's Search in the SLD-tree

Prolog builds the SLD-tree for a given query using the clauses in the program in the order in which they occur, in a depth-first manner: the leftmost branch in the SLD-tree is generated first. If this branch is infinite, Prolog will fail to find an answer even if there are other successful branches. For this reason, it is important to put first in the program the clauses that will stop the resolution process.

If during the traversal of the tree Prolog arrives to a failure leaf, it will go back (towards the root of the tree) to explore the remaining branches. This process is called *backtracking*.

Prolog usually stops after finding the first solution for a given query, but it will backtrack and continue traversing the tree (always in a depth-first search, from left to right) if we require more answers.

We could summarise Prolog's operational semantics as SLD-resolution with a depth-first search strategy and automatic backtracking.

Example 70 *Consider the program P defining the predicate* append:

```
append([],L,L).
append([X|L],Y,[X|Z]) :- append(L,Y,Z).
```

The goal

```
:- append(X,[1,2],U).
```

produces the answer: $\{X \mapsto [], U \mapsto [1, 2]\}$ *but if we change the order of the clauses in the program the same goal leads to an infinite computation. In this case there is no answer for the query, and eventually the interpreter will give an error message (out of memory space, because the leftmost branch of the SLD-tree that Prolog is trying to build is infinite).*

SLD-resolution has interesting computational properties:

1. It is refutation-complete: Given a Prolog program and a goal, if a contradiction can be derived, then SLD-resolution will eventually generate an empty resolvent.

2. It is independent of the computation rule: If there is an answer for a goal, SLD-resolution will find it whichever selection rule is employed for choosing the literals resolved upon.

However, the particular tree traversal strategy that Prolog uses is not complete. In the example above, we see that if we change the order of the clauses in the program, Prolog fails to find an answer, even if an empty resolvent can be generated by SLD-resolution. The problem is that this empty resolvent will be generated in a branch of the SLD-tree that Prolog does not build.

There is an easy way to obtain a refutation-complete implementation of SLD-resolution: using breadth-first search instead of depth-first search. However, there is a price to pay: a breadth-first search strategy will in general take more time to find the first answer. For this reason this strategy is not used in practice.

7.4 Exercises

1. (a) When is a substitution called the most general unifier of two atoms?

   (b) Give the most general unifier (if it exists) of the following atoms (recall that `[1,2]` is short for `[1|[2|[]]]`):

   i. `append([1,2],X,U)`, `append([Y|L],Z,[Y|R])`
   ii. `append([1,2],X,[0,1])`, `append([Y|L],Z,[Y|R])`
   iii. `append([],X,[0,1])`, `append([Y|L],Z,[Y|R])`
   iv. `append([],X,[0])`, `append([],[X|L],[Y])`

2. Show that the resolvent of the clauses

   P :- $A_1, \ldots, A_n$

   and

   :- $Q_1, \ldots, Q_m$

   is also a Horn clause.

3. Consider the program:

   `nat(s(X)) :- nat(X).`

   `nat(0).`

   and the query:

   `:- nat(Y).`

   (a) Write the complete SLD-resolution tree for this query.

   (b) Explain why Prolog will not find an answer for this query.

   (c) Change the program so that Prolog can find an answer.

4. Define in Prolog a binary predicate `member` such that `member(a,l)` is true if the element `a` is in the list `l`.

   What are the answers to the following queries? Draw the SLD-resolution tree for each one.

   (a) `:- member(1,[2,1,3]).`

   (b) `:- member(1,[2,3,4]).`

(c) :- member(1,[]).

5. What is the purpose of the *occur-check* in the unification algorithm?

6. Write a logic program for sorting a list of numbers (in ascending order), using the insertion sort algorithm.

   For this, you will need to define:

   - a predicate sort such that sort(L,L') holds if L' is a list containing the same elements as L but in ascending order;
   - a predicate insertion such that insertion(X,L,L') holds if X is a number, L is a sorted list (in ascending order) and L' is the result of inserting X in the corresponding place in the list L.

7. Consider the following program and query:

   Program:

   grandparent(X,Z) :- parent(X,Y),parent(Y,Z).

   parent(X,Y) :- mother(X,Y).

   parent(X,Y) :- father(X,Y).

   mother(eileen,alice).

   mother(alice,victoria).

   father(stephen,victoria).

   sister(alice,jan).

   Query:

   :-grandparent(eileen,Z).

   Write an SLD-resolution tree for this query.

   What are the answers to this query?

8. Consider the following program and queries:

   Program:

   even(0).

   even(s(s(X))) :- even(X).

   odd(s(0)).

   odd(X) :- even(s(X)).

   Queries:

   :- odd(s(s(0))).

```
:- odd(s(0)).
```

Write an SLD-resolution tree for each query.

We now replace the fourth clause of the program by:

```
odd(X) :- greater(X,s(0)), even(s(X)).
```

Write the clauses defining the predicate `greater` such that `greater(m,n)` holds when the number m is greater than n.

Give the SLD-tree for the query:

```
:-odd(s(0)).
```

with the modified program.

9. A graph is a set $V = \{a, b, c, \ldots\}$ of vertices and a set $E \subseteq V \times V$ of edges. We use the binary predicate `edge` to represent the edges: `edge(a,b)` means that there is an edge from a to b. In a directed graph the edges have a direction, so `edge(a,b)` is different from `edge(b,a)`. We say that there is a *path* from a to b if there is a sequence of one or more edges that allows us to go from a to b.

   (a) Write a Prolog program defining the predicate `path`.

   (b) Write a query to compute all the directed paths starting from a in the graph.

   (c) Write a query to compute all the directed paths in the graph.

Bibliography

[1] R. Bird. *Introduction to Functional Programming using Haskell.* Prentice Hall, 1998.

[2] G. Cousineau and M. Mauny. *The Functional Approach to Programming.* Cambridge University Press, 1998.

[3] J. Gosling, B. Joy, and G. Steele. *The Java Language Specification.* Addison-Wesley, Reading, MA, 1996.

[4] C. J. Hogger. *Introduction to Logic Programming.* APIC Studies in Data Processing series. Academic Press, 1984.

[5] IBM. *Preliminary Report, Specifications for the IBM Mathematical FORmula TRANslating System.* IBM Corporation, New York, 1954.

[6] B. W. Kernighan and D. M. Ritchie. *The C Programming Language.* Software Series. Prentice Hall, second edition, 1988.

[7] A. Martelli and U. Montanari. An efficient unification algorithm. *Transactions on Programming Languages and Systems,* 4(2):258–282, 1982.

[8] J. McCarthy, P. Abrahams, D. Edwards, T. Hart, and M. Levin. *LISP 1.5 Programmer's Manual, 2d ed.* MIT Press, Cambridge, MA, 1965.

[9] R. Milner. A theory of type polymorphism in programming. *Journal of Computer and System Sciences,* 17, 1978.

[10] R. Milner, M. Tofte, and R. Harper. *The Definition of Standard ML.* MIT Press, 1990.

[11] P. Naur. Report on the algorithmic language ALGOL 60. *Communications of ACM,* 3(5), 1960.

[12] H. R. Nielson and F. Nielson. *Semantics with Applications : A Formal Introduction.* Wiley, 1992.

[13] S. Peyton Jones and J. H. (eds). Standard libraries for the Haskell 98 programming language, 1998. `www.haskell.org/library/`.

[14] A. M. Pitts. Semantics of programming languages, 2002. Lecture Notes and Slides, Cambridge University.

[15] R. Plasmeijer and M. van Eekelen. Concurrent Clean Language Report (versions 1.3 and 2.0).
`http://www.cs.kun.nl/~clean/contents/contents.html`.

[16] G. Plotkin. A structural approach to operational semantics. Technical Report DAIMI FN-19, Aarhus University, 1981.

[17] J. A. Robinson. A machine-oriented logic based on the resolution principle. *Journal of the ACM*, 12(1):23–41, 1965.

[18] P. Roussel. PROLOG: Manuel de référence et d'utilisation, 1975. Research Report, Artificial Intelligence Team, University of Aix-Marseille, France.

[19] G. Sussman and G. Steele. Scheme: An interpreter for extended lambda calculus, 1975. MIT AI Memo 349.

[20] P. Weiss and X. Leroy. *Le Langage CAML.* Dunod, Paris, 1999.

[21] G. Winskel. *The Formal Semantics of Programming Languages.* Foundations of Computing. The MIT Press, Cambridge, Massachusetts, 1993.

[22] N. Wirth. The programming language Pascal. *Acta Informatica*, 1(1):35–63, 1971.

Index

Lightning Source UK Ltd.
Milton Keynes UK
07 April 2010

152441UK00002B/10/A